Programmed Learning Aid for

PRINCIPLES OF SALESMANSHIP

Programmed Learning Aid for

Principles of
SALESMANSHIP

RICHARD H. HOWLAND
Professor and Chairman of the Marketing Department
Northern Illinois University

Coordinating Editor
ROGER H. HERMANSON
The University of Maryland

LEARNING SYSTEMS COMPANY

A division of
Richard D. Irwin, Inc., Homewood, Illinois   60430

Canadian distribution through Irwin-Dorsey Limited, Georgetown, Ontario

ISBN 0-256-01261-X
Printed in the United States of America

1 2 3 4 5 6 7 8 9 0 K 8 7 6 5 4 3 2

FOREWORD

Each of the books comprising the Programmed Learning Aid Series is in programmed learning format to provide the reader with a quick, efficient, and effective means of grasping the essential subject matter.

The specific benefits of the programmed method of presentation are as follows:

1. It keeps the reader *active* in the learning process and increases his comprehension level.
2. Incorrect responses are *corrected immediately*.
3. Correct responses are *reinforced immediately*.
4. The method is *flexible*. Those who need more "tutoring" receive it because they are encouraged to reread frames in which they have missed any of the questions asked.
5. The method makes learning seem like a game.

The method of programming used in this PLAID on salesmanship and in most of the other PLAIDs is unique and simple to use. The reader begins by reading Frame 1¹ in Chapter 1. At the end of that frame he will answer the True-False questions given. To determine the correctness of his responses he merely turns the page and examines the answers given in Answer Frame 1¹. He is told *why* each statement is true or false. He should use his performance on the questions given as a measure of his understanding of all the materials in Frame 1¹. If he misses any of the questions asked, he is encouraged to reread Frame 1¹ before continuing on to Frame 2¹. This same procedure should be used throughout the book. Specific instructions are given throughout as to where to turn next to continue working the program.

The reader may desire to go through the PLAID a second time leaving out the programmed questions and answers. Or, he may desire to further test his understanding by going through it a second time answering all of the questions once again and rereading only those frames in which his comprehension is unsatisfactory.

I wish to express my appreciation to William G. Nickels, Assistant Professor of Marketing, University of Maryland, for his assistance in the programming of the PLAID.

The author of this PLAID on salesmanship has been a professor and university administrator for over twenty years. He has done consulting in the areas of selling and sales management for such companies as General Motors, Motorola, United Air Lines, Deluxe Check Printers, and other companies. He also serves as president of *Four-Way Selling*, which specializes in salesmanship and sales training programs. The author has written several books and numerous articles. I'm sure you will agree that he has presented the essential subject matter in a clear and concise manner.

ROGER H. HERMANSON
Coordinating Editor and Programmer

v

PREFACE

This programmed learning aid is designed to serve as an overall review guide. It may supplement another text or be the major source material for studying the principles and techniques of selling. It is also designed to meet the needs of students, and beginning and seasoned salesmen.

Writing a book on salesmanship always presents two problems. First, salesmanship is an art which is difficult to learn by reading alone. The theories and principles discussed must also be demonstrated and/or applied for the reader to fully understand and appreciate them. Second, there are many different types and levels of selling, and each sales presentation must be geared to varying types of buyers. Consequently, it is difficult to use examples which will apply in all cases with equal effectiveness. It is hoped that the reader will recognize these two limitations in reading and using this programmed guide. In addition to recognizing that simulated practice or actual experience in selling can help to enrich the material in this book, the reader should also recognize that the first step is to understand something about the theories, concepts, techniques, and processes involved in selling. Theory and actual or simulated practice complement each other and both approaches are necessary for learning about selling.

This programmed learning aid includes a topical outline of the course material, a table of contents, 18 chapters covering the whole array of selling topics, a glossary, and an index. Questions and answers appear throughout the PLAID and are designed to develop fuller understanding and to evaluate the reader's performance as he progresses. There is a review consisting of 37 questions for Chapters 1 to 9 inclusive, a second review for Chapters 10 to 18 inclusive, and a final comprehensive examination consisting of 74 questions covering Chapters 1 to 18. It is a complete and practical approach for studying salesmanship which gives the reader a better understanding of selling and also helps to improve his performance in terms of actual sales.

RICHARD H. HOWLAND

TOPICAL OUTLINE OF COURSE CONTENT

CONTENTS

chapter 1

SELLING: ITS DEVELOPMENT AND ROLE IN THE AMERICAN SOCIETY

Frame 1[1]

The applications of salesmanship

The Definitions Committee of the American Marketing Association defines selling as "the personal or impersonal process of assisting and/or persuading a prospective customer to buy a commodity or service or to act favorably upon an idea that has commercial significance to the seller." However, in actual practice the applications of salesmanship are much broader in scope, for it is an activity which permeates almost every avenue of human endeavor. The ability to convince people is a necessary skill for lawyers, teachers, ministers, politicians, and many others. It is a skill used by the doctor when he attempts to convince his patient that he should stop smoking; or a skill used by a mother when she explains to her young son that stealing is wrong. Actually, then, salesmanship is the ability to influence and convince others, and we practice it almost every day.

History and development of salesmanship

Selling as a function of business existed as early as 4000 B.C. when the Arabs traveled in caravans and traded their wares in Mesopotamia and Egypt. Early Greeks and Romans also traveled to foreign countries to market their goods. Selling during these days was accomplished mostly by bartering and haggling. People felt that it was wrong to make a profit by the exchange of goods and services, and anyone who engaged in such transactions was looked upon with contempt. This attitude toward selling changed somewhat during the Middle Ages when it was recognized that profits could be justified by the creation of time and place utilities.

During the 13th and 14th centuries, Italian merchants sold their products throughout Europe. The traveling salesman as we know him today, however, did not make his appearance until the latter half of the 18th century. Then, and on into the 19th century, England led the other countries in the use of traveling salesmen. During this period, many young men in America were also beginning their careers as traders, merchants, peddlers, or "drummers."

In the beginning, selling in the United States was confined to local areas. However, there were a few young men who traveled the countryside in order to expand their markets. Hires, for example, peddled root beer in Philadelphia; Heinz sold horseradish from a wheelbarrow; and Wrigley originally marketed his chewing gum out of a basket.

The early Yankee peddlers traveled from one community to another selling assorted small wares such as pots, pans, perfume, sewing supplies, spices, and so on. These men generally used high-pressure tactics to sell their merchandise. At the same time, trading posts and country stores were slowly springing up; and although most of these stores sold unbranded merchandise, some of them began building customer demand by branding their packing cases with a hot iron. This marked the beginning of the trademark in the United States.

The middle of the 19th century was characterized by great improvements in transportation and communications, and the great array of new inventions in machinery helped launch the mass production era. Hence, the local craftsman who had customers come to his shop for goods was replaced by machines which produced large quantities of goods. It therefore became necessary to seek markets in other areas, and the role of marketing in business was greatly expanded. This new era in marketing resulted in the decline of the "drummer," typically a friendly backslapper but also inclined to use unscrupulous and high-pressure tactics. Also, the old general or country store was replaced by the department store, the mail-order house and, later, by the chain store. The old-time practice of haggling was replaced by "one price to all"; manufacturers and wholesalers developed new marketing channels; private and national brands emerged; and advertising became a part of the selling process.

During the period from 1900 to 1950, our capacity to produce began to outstrip our ability to sell these goods and services. Attention therefore began to be concentrated on improving the art of selling and sales management. Such refinements as organized training programs, better selection of salesmen, bonuses, contests, premiums, motivational meetings, illustrated presentations, and other innovations were developed to help make the salesman more productive. For a brief period after World War II, a shortage of products and services created a seller's market. However, this situation was short-lived.

Today the salesman operates in an environment which is extremely competitive, highly refined, and considerably more professionalized than it used to be. The typical salesman of today is not a high-pressure huckster who attempts to sell the buyer something he does not need or want. On the contrary, his major objective is to satisfy and serve the customer in every respect, for in today's competitive economy the company must make repeat sales if it is to remain in business. We have shifted to a consumer-oriented economy, and it requires a much higher degree of professionalism and competency than previously existed.

Indicate whether each of the following statements is true or false by writing "T" or "F" in the space provided.

_____ 1. Broadly defined, salesmanship is the ability to convince people.

_____ 2. Selling as a function of business is a very modern development, since the ancient world saw making a profit on such activities as evil.

_____ 3. The United States led other countries in the use of traveling salesmen, and these salesmen, known as Yankee peddlers, were "soft-sell" types.

_____ 4. The improvements in machinery, transportation, and communications led to important changes in marketing.

_____ 5. Today's typical salesman uses high-pressure tactics.

Now turn to Answer Frame 1[1] on page 4 to check your responses.

Frame 2[1]

The contributions of selling

Salesmanship plays an important role in our lives. Among its functions in, and contributions to, our business and economic system are the following:

1. It has helped to make the United States one of the most productive economies in the world.
2. It has given our country the highest standard of living in the world.
3. It is the major objective of every business enterprise and the only function that generates

direct revenue and profits. In this sense, then, it is the heart of our business economy.

4. It helps to maintain the spirit of competition, which is the basis for a free enterprise system.
5. In today's mass society, "the world will not beat a path to your door," and selling becomes the bridge for introducing new products and services.
6. When a new product or service is introduced by a competitive firm, a company offering an established product or service will often rely on improved salesmanship to retain its share of the market.

New concepts in selling

Our economy has shifted from a "manufacturing-oriented" economy to a "marketing-oriented" economy. This means that we generally do not first design and manufacture a product and then decide how to market or sell it. Instead, we first carefully study the marketplace to determine what the consumer needs and wants. Selling and promotional strategies are also determined, and then the product is designed and manufactured in accordance with these factors. In applying this concept, the function of selling becomes more important in the total business environment and involves a greater degree of coordination with the other business functions.

Each year more and more companies are operating on the basis of this "marketing concept." Those who adopt this marketing approach make important changes in their methods, usually with improved results. They focus on satisfying the consumer, but they also zero in on the accomplishment of the company's objectives—increased sales volume, larger share of the market, but above all, if the company is to survive, adequate profits. All aspects of the business are integrated to achieve these goals. No longer is production allowed to become an end in itself or to dominate company policies.

In short, the marketing concept envisions a total system of operation in which satisfying the consumer leads to profitable sales. Satisfying the consumer is the means of achieving long-run as well as immediate profits. The customer, then, becomes the fulcrum supporting all the activities of the business. Implementation of this philosophy requires teamwork by all those in marketing research, product planning, sales forecasting, advertising, selling, physical distribution, sales analysis and control, and other related marketing activities. Selling plays a key role in this combined effort because a customer is not satisfied nor is a profit made until the product or service is actually sold.

Business today is also influenced by more competition, both domestically and from abroad. There are more rigid cost controls, and more and better information is now available regarding the products and services we buy. Furthermore, labor, material, and operating costs have greatly increased, and profit margins are therefore narrower. All of these conditions have made the work of the salesman more important and complex. Accordingly, selling today requires more knowledge and skill.

The modern salesman not only must be skillful in selling his product or service but must also be able to show the individual customer how to use the product or service in solving his particular needs or problems. If he sells a product to a merchant, he may also be required to show the merchant how to retail the product and be prepared to advise him on activities ranging from choosing a store location to developing inventory methods, preparing advertising, analyzing consumer behavior, setting prices, and others. With this expansion in the activities of selling, the modern salesman of today must be knowledgeable in many areas of business and be capable of adjusting to a multitude of varying circumstances.

Is salesmanship an art or a science?

To qualify as a science in the strictest sense, salesmanship would have to make greater use than it does of the "scientific method." This method proceeds in definite stages: first, data are gathered through observation; second, hypotheses are formulated through inductive reasoning; and third, the hypotheses are tested through further observation and *controlled* experiment. In science, the several variables involved in the experiment can be controlled, and the experiment will always produce the same result under the same

Answer frame 1[1]

1. True. Salesmanship is the ability to influence or convince others, and all of us practice it frequently.
2. False. Selling as a function of business existed as early as 4000 B.C. It is true that making a profit on such activities was frowned upon and caused those engaged in selling to be looked upon with contempt. But selling was still performed. During the Middle Ages the justification of profits for selling was recognized.
3. False. England led the other countries in the use of traveling salesmen. Also, the Yankee peddlers used high-pressure tactics in selling their merchandise.
4. True. These improvements led to mass production with their resulting need for mass marketing. The "one-price-to-all" policy evolved along with private and national brands, chain stores, new marketing channels, and advertising.
5. False. He must satisfy and serve the customer so that he can make repeat sales.

An attempt has been made in each frame to test the most important concepts within that frame. It is unlikely that this has been accomplished in every instance. Therefore, you should use your performance on the questions asked at the end of each frame as an indication of your comprehension of *all* the concepts in that frame. If you missed any of the above, you should restudy Frame 1[1] before turning to Frame 2[1] on page 2. You should use this same procedure throughout the PLAID.

Frame 2[1] continued

conditions no matter when, where, or by whom performed. For example, chemistry is a science in this sense because all the variables such as compounds, weight, and temperatures can be controlled with exact preciseness. Consequently, an experiment can be conducted today, tomorrow, next year, or even a hundred years from now and the same results can be obtained.

However, in selling, the several variables affecting the sale, such as customer behavior, competitive activity, the weather, and general economic conditions, cannot be controlled. Furthermore, each customer is different from all others in some way. Hence, each sales situation is uniquely different, and the salesman's approach must be varied according to the specific circumstances that prevail in each case. For these reasons selling is not a science and will remain an art as long as there are varying circumstances and invididual differences. But, this does not mean that the salesman can be careless and lackadaisical in his approach to selling.

On the contrary, the varied and ever-changing circumstances make it all the more necessary for him to be alert and well organized.

Must you be a born salesman or can salesmanship be taught and learned?

Some people still believe that in order to be a success in selling one must have a magnetic personality, a silver tongue, and a firm handshake. It is true that a person who possesses these qualities certainly will have the edge over one who does not. However, to say that you must be born with a certain set of traits to succeed in selling is as ridiculous as saying that you are born as a lawyer, a doctor, or a minister. All of these professions had to be learned through years of study and training. Salesmanship can also be learned. But to be a success at it, you must be able to discipline yourself and constantly strive to improve your performance.

Label each of the following statements as true or false.

_____ 1. If you build a better mousetrap, the world will beat a path to your door.

_____ 2. The United States has shifted from a "manufacturing-oriented" economy to a "marketing-oriented" economy.

_____ 3. Through careful analysis of the market and years of practice, salesmanship has become a science in the strict sense of the word.

_____ 4. People who lack the natural skills of a born salesman may learn these
skills by studying and practicing.

Now turn to Answer Frame 2[1] on page 6 to check your answers.

chapter 2

THE SALESMAN'S RESPONSIBILITIES AND QUALIFICATIONS

Frame 1[2]

His responsibility to the buyer

Successful selling does not end with getting the initial order; it builds volume by generating repeat orders that continue as long as the customer has a need for the product or service the salesman is selling. From this standpoint, the major objective of selling is to serve and satisfy the buyer. Outwitting the customer and putting something over on him for the sake of earning a commission is detrimental not only to the buyer but also to the salesman and his company as well. Such a sale creates a dissatisfied buyer; and if he is dissatisfied, there will be no repeat business. Selling today, therefore, emphasizes an approach which is genuinely "buyer oriented" and it begins and continues by fulfilling the customer's particular needs and wants.

His responsibility to the company

The salesman also has important responsibilities to his company. In many cases, he is the only contact the buyer has with the company and, therefore, becomes responsible for projecting the corporate image. He is also responsible for selling the product or service at a profit for the company. If he sells a product which pleases the buyer and earns him a commission but does not result in a profit for the company, he will not be a successful salesman. A company must make profits if it is to continue in business.

In addition to his selling duties, a salesman is responsible for filling out orders, completing reports, collecting market information in the field, and following through on customer service and

Answer frame 2¹

1. False. In today's mass society, the makers and users of new products and services are widely separated, and selling is the bridge that brings buyers and sellers together.
2. True. Today in the United States, firms first determine consumer wants and needs, then they produce what is desired and selling is coordinated with other business functions to solve customer needs.
3. False. Selling is an art, because each sales situation is uniquely different and the salesman's approach must vary according to the circumstances.
4. True. Salesmanship can be learned, but one must discipline himself to study and practice so that he may improve his performance.

If you missed any of the above, you should reread Frame 2¹ before beginning Chapter 2 on page 5.

Frame 1² continued

complaints. His responsibilities to the company then are fourfold:

a) He must do everything he can do to project a favorable image.
b) He must sell in such a manner as to produce reasonable profits for his company.
c) He must provide the company with reports and other related information.
d) He must follow through on customer service and complaints.

Qualifications for selling

The qualifications necessary for successful selling will vary with the type of product or service being sold. For example, the salesman who sells industrial equipment must know a great deal about designing, mechanical engineering, and current research in the field. On the other hand, the product knowledge and degree of preparation is less complex for the counter saleslady who sells handkerchiefs. Furthermore, although much has been written on this subject, no two companies will completely agree on the ranking of desirable traits necessary for successful selling. Nonetheless, the traits or characteristics mentioned in the remainder of this chapter frequently are listed and certainly will help a person to be a more effective salesman.

Indicate whether each of the following statements is true or false by writing "T" or "F" in the space provided.

_____ 1. The primary concern of a salesman is to get the initial order by "putting over a deal."

_____ 2. Salesmen should only be concerned with selling products which please customers and not be concerned with corporate profits.

_____ 3. Salesmen have other duties to the company besides selling goods and services at a profit.

_____ 4. There are certain traits or characteristics that will help any salesman to be more effective.

Now turn to Answer Frame 1² on page 8 to check your responses.

Frame 2²

Product knowledge. The first requirement for successful selling is product knowledge. The salesman is responsible for explaining the benefits and uses of his product or service, showing how it fulfills or solves the prospect's needs or problems, and answering the prospect's questions and objections. If he is poorly prepared or inadequately informed about his product, he will do a poor job in meeting these responsibilities. It will also impair his ability to gain the prospect's respect and confidence. Hence, successful selling begins with product knowledge. The salesman needs to know something about the history and organization of the company; how the product is made; its benefits and uses; how it compares with competitor products; and how to operate, maintain, or care for it. He should be well informed as to prices; different sizes, styles, or models; payment methods; shipping or delivery procedures; guarantees and warranties; and service and adjustment policies.

Positive attitude. Selling is not an occupation that is completely devoid of tension, frustration, and insecurity. On top of this, a sufficient number of social and economic problems plague our society to drive almost anyone to the brink of despair. However, if we approach our problems with a negative or defeatist attitude, we generally are licked at the start. Our attitude determines our behavior; and our behavior, in turn, will determine our performance. In practice, "a positive attitude" means to minimize worry about problems and to concentrate on ways and means to solve them. It means to be optimistic rather than pessimistic. If the salesman is to make the prospect positive minded about his product or service, he himself must possess and manifest this feeling.

Enthusiasm. Enthusiasm is the strong desire and interest a person feels when he believes that what he is doing or experiencing is exciting and worthwhile. It is a feeling of strongly liking something and being fervently absorbed in it. A salesman who sells with enthusiasm is alive and dynamic. It is vital for him to feel this way; for if he has little enthusiasm for his product, it is extremely difficult, if not impossible, for him to convince the buyer of its merits. Enthusiasm is comparable to the fuel which fires the machine. It is a necessary trait for effective and successful selling, and as Lincoln once said, "Nothing great was ever accomplished without enthusiasm."

Confidence. Confidence is a belief that you can achieve what you wish to accomplish. It is self-assurance, reliance, and faith. If you want to do something but believe you can't, the chances that you will fail are much greater than if you approach your task with a determination to succeed.

In order to develop confidence in the buyer, the salesman must first have confidence in himself. Inevitably, the environment in which selling is done will challenge the salesman, and if he lacks confidence in himself or his product, he will generally be unsuccessful.

Liking people. A salesman has to like people, because products and services are sold through and to people. And liking people means much more than just being friendly. For the salesman it means continuing to like people even when he believes they are wrong or when they make him discouraged or angry. Liking people also means trying to understand them, and doing everything you possibly can to help them.

Empathy. Empathy is "putting yourself in the other fellow's shoes." It means a sensitivity to the feelings and interest of others. Empathy also involves skill in analyzing how others are reacting to what you are saying and doing. A strong sense of empathy is an important quality for successful selling; and a salesman who lacks it is at a serious disadvantage in attempting to convince the prospect on the merits of his product or service.

Ability to communicate and persuade. The ability to communicate involves four phases:

a) Getting the person's *attention*.
b) Getting him to *understand* you.
c) Getting him to *appreciate* and *believe* you.
d) And finally, getting him *to do* or *act upon* what you suggest.

In this sense, communication is the ability to persuade and convince others. It is a very important skill in successful selling and includes a good voice, the ability to listen and observe, appropriate speech and grammar, acceptable manners and gestures, effective planning and organization, and showmanship.

Determination and persistence. The number of sales a salesman makes usually is directly dependent upon the number of calls he makes. Also, the number of calls will usually outnumber the sales, and in some cases the call-sales ratio may be as great as 5 to 1 or even higher depending upon the product or service being sold. In addition, several repeat calls on a particular prospect must often be made before a sale is achieved. To make and keep on making the large number of calls that success demands, a salesman must possess a

Answer frame 1²

1. False. Successful selling means getting the initial order *and* continuing repeat sales by being "buyer oriented" and creating satisfied buyers.
2. False. Salesmen are responsible for selling products and services at a profit for the company, or else the company might go out of business.
3. True. In addition to their sales duties, salesmen must project a favorable image for the firm, provide reports and other information, and follow through on customer service and complaints.
4. True. Although no two companies agree on the ranking of desirable traits for salesmen, there are some traits or characteristics that are mentioned most frequently as being helpful.

If you missed any of the above, you should restudy Frame 1² before beginning Frame 2² on page 6.

Frame 2² continued

high degree of determination and persistence. He cannot allow himself to become discouraged and must continue his efforts until his objective is achieved. Not too many people can do this, for it is much easier to find excuses or to wait for buyers to come to them. However, such an approach will seldom work; for no matter how good your product or service might be, prospects generally will not beat a path to your door. Many other choices are usually available to the buyer, and the market for a given product is usually too competitive for this to happen. Consequently, the salesman must work in a determined and persistent manner in order to be successful.

Self-starter. Being a self-starter means having the capacity to do things on your own with little or no supervision from others. The salesman has a high degree of freedom, as he generally works alone, with little interference or supervision; and in certain types of selling, the salesman is completely free each day to decide when he will work, where he will work, and what he will do. Many find this freedom to be one of the advantages of pursuing a career in selling. However, it also means that the person out in the field selling is responsible for supervising himself. Those who lack initiative or are incapable of disciplining themselves will fail as salesmen. The work of selling is demanding and involves considerable time and effort if one is to succeed. Consequently, it requires a person who can operate on his own with little or no supervision; a person who can organize and complete his own work schedules. In short, selling is a highly individualized occupa-

tion; and in order to succeed in it, one should have a high degree of personal initiative and be a self-starter.

Sense of humor. As previously mentioned, considerable time and effort is often spent on calls which may never result in sales. Also, buyers, by what they say and do, can sometimes discourage or frustrate a salesman. It is difficult and trying to operate in such an environment, and a salesman without a sense of humor can easily be overcome by these circumstances. With a sense of humor, however, he can see the lighter side of human nature and is less apt to take himself too seriously. He must learn how to live with frustration, how to be friendly in unfriendly environments, and how to adjust to discouragement and failure. A sense of humor will, therefore, not only help him to survive, but will also help him to be a more likable person.

Creativity. All buyers tend to be different, and each sales situation requires a somewhat different approach. Furthermore, in an economy of increased competition, product qualities and prices tend to become more similar. In such an environment, the creative ability of the salesman becomes an important factor in securing the sale. To be creative means being alert and looking for new approaches to solving persistent problems. It involves constant experimentation in an attempt to find new ideas to help and serve the buyer. Selling is an art of adaptation to varying circumstances, and there is a great need in today's marketplace for the creative salesman.

Appearance. Much that has been written on

appearance has been erroneous and based on individual prejudice. Salesmen vary in height, weight, and physical looks. To be successful, one does not have to be tall; to be trusted, one does not have to have blue eyes. More important than inherited physical traits are the actions the salesman takes to keep neat, well groomed, and well dressed. Although successful salesmen will vary considerably in height, weight, and physical looks, almost all of them will be neat and properly dressed.

Good health.   Good health is the most precious gift a man can possess. The salesman should watch his diet, exercise regularly, rest a sufficient number of hours, and be careful not to abuse his body. Such care will prolong his life and also help him to be a more effective and productive salesman.

Poise and composure.   The person who has poise and composure is well controlled and well mannered. He does not "fly off the handle" and is able to "keep his cool" in trying situations. He is also tactful, and has an air about him that instills confidence and respect in those who observe him. Hence, poise and composure are qualities necessary not only to be an effective leader but to be an effective salesman as well.

Sincerity and honesty.   Sincerity means taking a genuine interest in serving the buyer. This is a quality that all prospects look for and attempt to measure in the salesman. If the buyer feels that the salesman is insincere, he will lack confidence in what the salesman says or does. Accordingly, it will be extremely difficult, if not impossible, for the salesman to convince the prospect that he should buy his product or service. Sincerity must be real and genuine. It cannot be faked, for prospects can consciously or unconsciously feel it. Honesty is closely related with sincerity and requires that the salesman be truthful in what he says and does for the customer. It means being upright in your activities as a salesman and selling as you would like to be sold.

Developing necessary qualifications

Some qualifications are easier to develop or teach than others. For example, a salesman can learn about his product, can be taught how to dress well, can learn proper grammar, and how to speak effectively. However, developing such qualifications as creativity, sincerity, being a self-starter, and determination and persistence are extremely difficult to teach, and in some cases, even impossible to teach. These latter qualifications present more serious problems for sales managers, and continued training is necessary to develop or improve them.

Label each of the following statements as true or false.

_____ 1.   The salesman should worry about his problems.

_____ 2.   The most successful salesmen are sensitive to the feelings and interests of others.

_____ 3.   Most customers are sold on the first sales call.

_____ 4.   Most salesmen are carefully supervised and have set schedules and duties.

_____ 5.   Successful salesmen learn one sales presentation and perfect it, and have little need to adapt to different buyers.

_____ 6.   The necessary qualifications and characteristics for becoming a successful salesman can all be taught to any individual.

Now check your answers by turning to Answer Frame 2² on page 10.

Answer frame 2²

1. False. The "right mental attitude" is to minimize worry and to concentrate on the positive aspects of solving problems.
2. True. Salesmen who have empathy, or the ability to analyze how others are reacting to what they are saying or doing, have a tremendous advantage in attempting to convince prospects of the merits of products and services.
3. False. It often requires several repeat calls before a sale is achieved, and in some cases the call-sales ratio may be as great as 5 to 1 or even higher.
4. False. Salesmen generally have a great deal of freedom and are not closely supervised. This means that they must supervise themselves and have a high degree of personal initiative.
5. False. All buyers tend to be different, and each sales situation requires a somewhat different approach. Salesmen must be creative, which means that they must be alert and look for new approaches to solving problems. Selling is an art of adapting to varying circumstances.
6. False. Some of them can, but others like creativity, sincerity, being a self-starter, and so on, are extremely difficult to teach, and in some cases, even impossible to teach.

If you missed any of the above, you should reread Frame 2² before beginning Chapter 3.

chapter 3

SELLING AS A CAREER

Frame 1[3]

Rewards of selling

Selling offers many career opportunities, for there are many different types and levels of selling. A person can sell a product or a service; he can sell to wholesalers, retailers, or ultimate consumers; and the product or service he sells can be technical or nontechnical. Methods for paying the salesman are also more varied than in many other types of jobs. He can be paid on a straight commission basis, a straight salary, or a combination of these two methods with many variations. In many selling jobs, earnings are unlimited and geared to the ability of the individual. In general, salesmen will receive significantly higher salaries than other business workers, particularly after they have become established and built up a clientele.

Another very important advantage of selling is that it is one of the main roads for promotion or advancement within the company. This is generally true because selling is the only business function which generates direct revenue and profits. Accounting, finance, production, general management, personnel administration, and other related business activities are all expense operations. However, nothing happens until the product or service is sold; and the success or failure of all these business activities are measured by what happens in selling. This is why it receives major attention and is the hub or pivot point of all business activity.

Work in selling is varied, challenging, and interesting. There is continuous contact with many different types of people, and each sales situation is uniquely different. No two customers are the same, and most products and services are constantly changed and improved to meet the varying demands of the marketplace. Almost every day there are new challenges and opportunities which make the work of the salesman very dynamic and interesting. He also gains considerable pride and personal satisfaction in representing a reputable company and in helping customers solve their problems.

A career in selling also provides considerable freedom and independence in comparison with many other types of jobs in business. A field salesman does not automatically begin each day at 8 A.M. and end it at 5 P.M. Nor does he punch a timeclock and work under the daily supervision of a boss. On the contrary, as mentioned in Chapter 2, in many types of selling the salesman has complete freedom in determining when he will work, where he will work, how long, whom he will call on, and what he will do. Of course, he must periodically report to a sales manager, and his performance is carefully evaluated. He is generally rewarded in proportion to his abilities.

Finally, a successful salesman has a skill which is highly transferable and is in constant demand. If he can sell one product or service well, with a little training he is generally capable of selling other products or services. The need for selling is universal; for although buyers will vary, they still buy many of the same products and services regardless of where they live.

Disadvantages of selling

As with all types of work, selling has some disadvantages. Many people dislike the high degree of persistence and personal discipline which is necessary for success in selling. The job requires time, training, and demands considerable stick-to-itiveness and the ability to shrug off rebuffs and disappointments, and many beginning salesmen do not have the necessary patience and determination to stay with it. There can also be uncertainty and insecurity in selling, for earnings are largely dependent upon the actions others take and the acceptance they give the salesman. Competition is always a threat, and general economic conditions, such as unemployment or rising prices, can unfavorably affect the earning power of the salesman. Some people, therefore, prefer a form of work which is more secure and stable.

In addition, some aspects of selling are lonely and monotonous. Sometimes great distances must be traveled, and the salesman may be away from home for several days. Also, long periods of time are sometimes spent in waiting to see prospective buyers. Work in selling can be very discouraging, for in the majority of cases more sales will be lost than gained.

However, the advantages of selling certainly outweigh its disadvantages for many people, and it provides considerable opportunity for personal satisfaction to those who have the necessary ability and determination to succeed.

Types of selling careers

Selling jobs can be classified in a number of different ways. Selling may be characterized as part time or full time; or as to whether it involves negotiation or competitive bidding; whether it is routine or creative; whether physical products or services are sold. Classifications may also be made according to the method of compensation—whether straight salary, commission, or salary and commission.

In characterizing sales duties, the nature of the buyer may be emphasized, particularly whether buying to consume or to resell. The buyers may be wholesalers and retailers who purchase for resale. They may be purchasing agents who buy materials which are processed and sold in a different form; or they may be ordinary people or professional men who use the product themselves.

Along these lines, the Sales Marketing Executives–International, Inc., has developed the following six classifications:

1. Consumer route. The job of the consumer route man is to sell and deliver goods to a list of consumer customers. The products are usually such staples as milk, bread, and laundry.
2. Business route. Salesmen on a business route sell and deliver such products or services as office, factory, and store supplies, production materials, and so on to a predetermined list of business customers.
3. Consumer specialties. The salesman of consumer specialties engages in door-to-door selling and handles such products or services as life insurance, household products, cosmetics, appliances, siding and insulation, and other related products. He often does "missionary" work.
4. Business specialties. The salesman of business specialties operates like the consumer specialty salesman except he sells products or services to business establishments and is likely to do more creative selling. These salesmen handle such items as business machines, business insurance, advertising, and management training services.
5. Retail. The retail salesman does not go to the customer; the customer comes to him at a fixed place of business where he sells goods or services over the counter. Items commonly sold in this manner are clothing, household furnishings, automobiles, and appliances.
6. Industrial. The industrial salesman generally must have a technical or engineering training. He sells such products as heavy equipment, machine installations, and product supplies.

Still another common way of classifying the salesman's job is according to the nature of his employer—whether a manufacturer, a wholesaler, or a retailer.

It can be seen that there are many different types of selling jobs. Even those selling jobs within the same category can vary greatly as to the level of work and training required. Hence, there is considerable opportunity in selling; and the area pursued will greatly depend upon to whom the product or service is sold, the salesman's interests, his level of education and training, and his particular abilities.

Scope of selling in the United States

In 1890 there were slightly more than 264,000 persons engaged in selling in the United States. However, by 1970 this number had expanded to 5,028,000 which comprised 8.8 percent of the total working force. During this 80-year period the population had increased 3.2 times, whereas the increase in sales personnel had increased more than 19 times. This dramatic increase illustrates the shift to a "marketing-oriented" economy and the increased importance of selling in the total business environment.

Indicate whether each of the following statements is true or false by writing "T" or "F" in the space provided.

_____ 1. In general, salesmen receive higher salaries than other business workers, and in many cases there is also greater opportunity for advancement.

_____ 2. Salesmen have a skill which is highly transferable from one firm to another and is in constant demand.

_____ 3. Because the work is creative and rewarding, there are few disadvantages to salesmanship as a career.

_____ 4. There are many different types of sales jobs which vary greatly as to the level of work and the training required.

Now turn to Answer Frame 1[3] on page 14 to check your responses.

Answer frame 1³

1. True. Salesmen often receive higher salaries because they generate direct revenue and profit, and this often leads to greater opportunity for advancement.
2. True. If a salesman can sell one product or service well, he is generally capable of selling other products or services if he is properly trained. The need for selling is universal, so there is always a demand for skilled salesmen.
3. False. As with any job, selling has some disadvantages such as the discouragement of making many calls with no results, long-distance travel away from home, insecurity of earnings, and the need for persistence and personal discipline.
4. True. There has been a tremendous increase in the number of salesmen in our economy and in the kind of work they do. The sales job varies from over-the-counter retail sales to highly complex industrial sales. Each job requires different educational and skill requirements.

If you missed any of the above, you should restudy Frame 1³ before beginning Chapter 4.

chapter 4

MOTIVATION AND CONSUMER BEHAVIOR

Frame 1⁴

What is motivation?

It is characteristic of all human beings to have *needs* and *wants*, which when unsatisfied lead to tensions or *drives*. These drives toward relief of the tensions created by unsatisfied needs furnish the motivation—the activating forces—that determine and explain consumer behavior.

To be effective in his work, the salesman must be able to analyze and understand consumer behavior and the motives that underlie it. What influences a particular customer to buy a particu-

lar good or service? If the salesman understands these motivating influences, he will be in a stronger position to sell. Strictly speaking, the salesman does not sell a product or service, but rather he changes the consumer's mind about the product or service. The product and salesman remain the same, and it is the buyer's mind that must be changed. People buy products for what they will do for them, not for the product in and of itself. It is necessary, then, to study the behavior of consumers and to determine why they buy.

A great deal has been written about consumer

behavior in the past two decades, and this vast subject can only be touched upon lightly in this brief chapter. There are also varying theories and philosophies regarding consumer behavior, and researchers in this area are not in common agreement.

No two customers are identical

The first thing to recognize about consumer behavior is that no two individuals are exactly the same. People tend to have differing degrees of traits such as optimism, confidence, aggressiveness, conservatism, and so on. Not only do people differ from one another, but the same person can be different under different circumstances. Changes in the weather, changes in time, and many other physical conditions can attract or distract a person's attention. How a person feels will influence his behavior. Whether he is happy or unhappy, alert or sleepy, relaxed or tense will greatly affect what he perceives and does. His use of alcohol, drugs, or medicine can produce changes in his behavior. And such incentives as praise, recognition, and reward usually will elicit a greater degree of response. Under varying conditions such as these, the salesman should carefully analyze the total selling situation to determine the best approach to use.

Basic kinds of motives

Although the terminology varies and there is no general agreement on how many basic motives there are, writers in this area generally see the consumer responding to three basic types of motives. The first of these classifications is *physiological*. These motives are related to the physical needs of the body and include those arising out of sex, hunger, thirst, and the desire for comfort. The second is *psychological*. These motives are largely subjective and include such motives as pride and fear. And the third is *sociological*. These motives are related to man's social status, including motives arising from the urges or needs for conformity, recognition, and prestige.

Some writers have pointed out that motives can be arranged as a hierarchy, with those needs the consumer regards as most important, and will try to satisfy first, at the top and the others that

can wait listed in turn below. The psychologist Abraham Maslow saw five levels of needs, which he listed in ascending order as follows:

1. Physiological needs.
2. Need for safety.
3. Need to belong, to love and be loved.
4. Desire for esteem and status.
5. Need for "self-actualization."

Maslow interpreted the need for self-actualization as a desire to find and fulfill the true self to the highest degree possible. He realized that this need came later in the hierarchy of needs after the others had been met.

Primary, selective, and patronage motives

Motives can also be classified as *primary, selective,* or *patronage*. A *primary* motive is related to those particular factors which motivate a person to choose one general type of product or service over another. For example, a man may simultaneously wish to purchase a new shotgun and storm windows. However, he usually doesn't have a sufficient amount of money to purchase both; consequently he must choose one over the other. In the case of the family man, although he wants to buy a new shotgun, he may decide that it is more important and sensible to buy storm windows for his home. Such considerations as the comfort of other family members, reduced heating bills, and increased value of his home may cause him to choose the storm windows over the shotgun and are referred to as primary buying motives. They relate to the type, kind, or class of product or service that will be purchased. *Selective* motives, on the other hand, are those that determine the consumer's choice of a brand. Once he has decided to purchase storm windows, he must next decide on the particular brand. Finally, *patronage* motives come into play. They involve decisions regarding the particular retailer or dealer from whom the product or service will be purchased.

Product motives

Consumer choice can also be influenced by the physical qualities or psychological attractiveness of the product. Such factors as design, color, size, quality, package, or price of the product can greatly influence or motivate the purchaser. For example, in designing packages, curved lines and fancy packages are generally thought to appeal to women, while straight lines and more functional packaging is considered more appropriate for products sold to men. With reference to color, red will normally attract more attention than green. And in promoting the cool taste of a cigarette, green and blue colors are frequently used.

The size of the container can also be an important motivating factor. Many shoppers select a larger size container because they can usually get more for their money by buying in larger quantities and it reduces the number of shopping trips. In addition, with our higher standard of living there is an increased emphasis on quality, but at the same time the product must be competitively priced. All of these factors can influence the purchase of a product, and they vary from one person to another. Product motives may also be thought of as economic or rational, as in the considerations of package size and price discussed in the preceding paragraph, or they may be classified as emotional. These classifications will be treated further on page 18.

Consumer behavior is also influenced by the type of product being sought. For example, such products as cigarettes, bread, meat, fruits and vegetables, gasoline, and toothpaste are classified as *convenience* goods. These products are frequently consumed on a daily or weekly basis, are available in many stores which are located near the consumer, are competitively priced, and are generally intensively advertised—particularly national brands.

Shopping goods, on the other hand, are such items as dresses, sport jackets, appliances, furniture, and automobiles. These products (in comparison with convenience goods) are consumed less frequently, are available in fewer outlets which are generally located further away from the consumer, and have greater variances in quality and price. The unit value of these products is also higher and often represents a sizable investment—particularly in the case of purchasing an automobile, furniture, or a major appliance. Consequently, the consumer plans these purchases more carefully and will usually compare or do considerable shopping before a final decision is made.

Specialty goods are products which have very special and unique characteristics. The consumer generally will "go out of his way" to purchase such products, and usually is reluctant to accept substitutes. A certain blend of pipe tobacco, an exceptionally fine camera, pastry products which are made in a special way, and rare woods which are available only from a certain area of the country are examples of products which are classified as specialty goods. In summary, the salesman should know the particular classification of his product and what effect its characteristics might have on influencing consumer behavior.

Indicate whether each of the following statements is true or false by writing "T" or "F" in the space provided.

_____ 1. Most products are *bought* by consumers rather than *sold* by salesmen.

_____ 2. Salesmen may use the same basic appeal to everyone because most people have the same needs.

_____ 3. Researchers do not agree on how many basic buying motives there are.

_____ 4. Consumer choice is influenced by other factors besides the sales talk.

Now turn to Answer Frame 1[4] on page 18 to check your responses.

Frame 2[4]

Positive versus negative motives

When the salesman emphasizes benefits or satisfactions that will be obtained from buying the product, he is emphasizing the positive approach. On the other hand, if he refers to a problem which the consumer wants to eliminate or avoid, he is using a negative approach. In selling life insurance, the salesman can emphasize the retirement benefits—this would be positive motivation. Or, he could emphasize the negative approach by referring to the financial difficulties a widow would have if her husband died and were inadequately insured. In selling a tire, the salesman can emphasize the positive by referring to its trouble-free qualities and the long mileage it will give. Or he can emphasize the negative by pointing out the dangers of traveling at high speed and having a blowout. The negative approach is based on problems and fears. Both approaches are effective, depending upon the product or service being sold and the consumer's particular circumstances. However, recent research by psychologists has revealed that man generally responds more favorably to a positive appeal than to a negative one.

Basic versus acquired wants

Motivation can also be analyzed from the standpoint of basic versus acquired wants. Almost everyone has the same basic wants, and they are generally uniform for all human beings. Psychologists differ as to the number of basic wants they identify, and the following ones are representative of those most frequently mentioned.

Love. Each of us has a basic need to love and be loved by others. The urge to appeal to the opposite sex plays a major role in our lives and influences our actions as consumers. Man also is concerned about the welfare of those he loves and usually assumes the responsibility for caring, protecting, and providing for them. Many parents not only provide a home for their children, but also labor to put them through college and even "help them out" in later life.

Food and shelter. Food and shelter are absolute essentials for living. There is a great range of differences in these needs varying from a dish of rice to a sirloin steak and from a simple hut to a stately manor. Nonetheless, we need food to live and work, and shelter to protect us from the elements.

Safety and security. Man wishes to avoid or eliminate anything that endangers or threatens his life. This basic urge manifests itself by his purchasing all forms of insurance, and in protecting himself and others through laws, support for police and fire protection, and other governmental services.

Achieve and accomplish. Most people strive to achieve and be recognized for something. They desire to be proud of what they do or accomplish. Attention, praise, and prestige are important motivating factors in our lives. In all things he undertakes, man basically wants to succeed rather than fail. He constantly seeks new challenges and is motivated by a strong desire to master them. Climbing a mountain, conquering space, breaking records, and fulfilling one's ambitions are common examples of this basic want.

Approval and acceptance. It is common for all of us to seek approval and acceptance by others. We generally try to avoid criticism and ridicule. Our need for approval, therefore, causes us to conform and imitate, rather than to deviate from social convention.

Leisure and relaxation. In addition to working and achieving, man also seeks rest, relaxation, pleasure, and fun. The increase in his leisure time and increased pressures of living have greatly influenced this need. Hundreds of recreational and avocational opportunities are available to him including golfing, fishing, hunting, skiing, reading, watching athletic events, gardening, and many other activities.

Need for health and survival. Maintaining good health is a major concern of man, and he will normally do everything in his power to avoid death. He also seeks to be free from fear, frustration, and pain. Millions of dollars are spent each year on research to find cures for common diseases and to lengthen his life. To live a long and happy life is a wished for goal of almost everyone.

Acquired or learned wants are further refined, and therefore become secondary or selective wants which vary with the person's background and cultural environment. Every man has the basic need for play and recreation, but the specific form it takes will vary considerably. For example, one man may fulfill this want by staying at home and reading a book. Another may attend a baseball or football game, and still another may fulfill this want by going on a lion hunt in Africa. Hence, the basic wants are common to all men, but the acquired wants will be different.

Answer frame 1[4]

1. True. Strictly speaking, salesmen do not sell products or services; rather, the consumer buys them. Therefore, it is necessary to understand consumers and why they buy.
2. False. People not only differ from one another, but the same person may react differently under different circumstances. Salesmen must vary their appeals according to the circumstances and needs of each customer.
3. True. Although there is no general agreement about buying motives, it is believed that at least three are basic: physiological (needs of the body), psychological (such as pride and fear), and sociological (the need to belong).
4. True. Consumer behavior is influenced by the product itself (design, color, size, price, package, and so on), by the type of product (convenience, shopping, or specialty good), and by the information provided by the salesman.

If you missed any of the above, you should restudy Frame 1[4] before beginning Frame 2[4] on page 16.

Frame 2[4] continued

Emotional versus rational motives

As mentioned in connection with product motives, consumer behavior can be viewed as being either emotional or economic or rational. Emotional motives are generally those which are based on feelings, are impulsive, and are not carefully planned in advance. Rational or economic motives, on the other hand, are more likely to be based on objective analysis and carefully planned. Examples of emotional motives would be those based on satisfaction of the senses, preservation of the species, love, pride, fear, emulation, sociability, acceptance, curiosity, and so on. Examples of rational motives would be those based on factors such as economy, efficiency in operation, durability, dependability, and others.

Difficulties in analyzing motives

In order to sell effectively, the salesman usually must be able to determine the motives of his potential customers. Sometimes this is relatively easy to do, but at other times it may be extremely difficult. For example, a person may not be aware of the true reasons why he is interested in purchasing a particular product or service. A buyer may tell himself and the salesman that he wishes to buy a new car because his old one is costing him too much for repairs. However, the real reason may be that he feels inferior and wishes to impress a certain young lady by buying a new car. The salesman must realize that stated reasons are not always the real reasons. A person may sometimes believe he knows why he is interested in buying a particular product or service, but actually he is unaware of his true motives; or in some cases he may be aware of his true motives, but is unwilling to disclose them. How many women would admit that they were buying a new dress in order to attract the attention of men? Or how many men would admit that they use a certain product in order to give themselves more masculinity? Thus, the salesman must understand human behavior and be careful in interpreting what the buyer says.

Finally, the salesman should remember that it is often a combination of motives with varying priorities that motivate people to buy. Two housewives will buy a vacuum cleaner to keep their homes clean. However, in addition to this basic need, one bought the cleaner because it was like the one her mother had, and she also liked the salesman because he reminded her of her own son. The other woman bought the cleaner because it was easy to handle, and it was also a better one than her neighbor had. Buying motives can vary greatly, and often no two people will buy a particular product or service for identical reasons. The salesman should be constantly aware of this and should adapt his presentation to the prospect's particular motives whenever possible.

Theories of motivation

In their text *Salesmanship: Principles and Methods*, Carlton A. Pederson and Milburn D. Wright have pointed out that theories of buyer motivation are basically of three types. An examination of the literature reveals that there are three different theories of motivation. The first is the *"mental-states"* theory, which maintains that the buyer's mind passes through successive stages during the buying process. These stages generally are "attention, interest, desire, action, and satisfaction." The second is the *"appeal-response"* or *"buying-decisions"* theory, which maintains that the buyer makes a number of separate decisions in

response to the appeals or stimuli presented by the salesman. The third theory is called the *"problem-solution"* theory. This theory states that the wants, needs, or problems of the buyer should be the salesman's frame of reference; and he gears his presentation to showing how his product or service will fulfill these wants or solve these problems. According to this latter theory, the salesman does not sell a product or service but rather he sells solutions to problems. Therefore, the more benefits his product can give, the more likely he is to make the sale.

Regardless of which theory the salesman may accept, he should recognize that there are different theories for analyzing motivation, and new discoveries are made each year which will help him to better understand the consumer he serves.

Label each of the following statements as true or false.

_____ 1. Psychologists agree that man generally responds more favorably to a positive appeal than a negative one.

_____ 2. People have basic wants that are uniform for almost everyone, but they also have acquired wants that vary considerably from individual to individual.

_____ 3. In order to determine why a customer wants a product, the salesman has only to ask the customer directly.

_____ 4. People always have a major reason for buying a product that is clear in their mind.

Now turn to Answer Frame 2⁴ on page 20 to check your answers.

Frame 3⁴*

Perception

Perception is an important factor affecting the behavior of consumers. It is the process of becoming aware of something through the senses of seeing, hearing, touching, tasting, smelling, and internal sensing. In relating to his environment, each person's needs, cultural background, past experiences, mental readiness, and motives will have an effect in determining how a given stimu-

lus is perceived, even though the stimulus is the same in all cases. For example, a jackknife may be perceived by a youngster as a toy, by his mother as an object for possible injury, and by the minister as an instrument which promotes violence and killing. How it is perceived greatly depends upon who the perceiver is and his particular frame of reference. No two persons are likely to perceive the same stimulus in exactly the same way. Each individual sees what he wants to see, making perception a subjective and individualized process.

Perception is also selective, for often we are unable to comprehend or interpret all the sensations that converge on the senses at any given time. When a person looks down an aisle in a

---

* The discussion in Frame 3⁴ of psychological aspects of consumer behavior is based to some extent on G. Glenn Walters and W. Paul, *Consumer Behavior: An Integrated Framework* (Homewood, Ill.: Richard D. Irwin, Inc., 1970), chaps. 16–17.

Answer frame 2⁴

1. True. Salesmen are usually more successful when they stress positive benefits, such as the satisfactions received from using a product, than they are when they dwell on negative factors, such as the dangers or problems resulting from not using the product.
2. True. Man has certain basic wants such as approval, comfort, food, mastery over obstacles, safety, and survival. Man also has acquired or learned wants. A salesman must determine how he can satisfy his customers' acquired wants as well as his basic wants.
3. False. Salesmen must realize that the reasons given by a customer for wanting a product are not necessarily the real reasons. The salesman must look for hidden reasons in order to fully satisfy the customer's needs.
4. False. It is often a combination of reasons that motivate people to buy. These reasons are complex and difficult to analyze. A salesman must be flexible and try to plan his presentation to meet the prospects' different motives.

If you missed any of the above, you should reread Frame 2⁴ before turning to Frame 3⁴ on page 19.

Frame 3⁴ continued

supermarket, he does not see the hundreds of items that are actually present. This is because the human mind generally is unable to absorb everything at once, and it selects those items which are of immediate importance.

In addition, perception is generally of short duration. When we listen to a particular piece of music, we may respond to it very strongly; but when it is ended, our attention is quickly diverted to other things, and the music fades from our minds.

Finally, perception is a summarizing experience. Consumers receive many varying sensations and put them together into a single, meaningful whole. For example, the brand name, special features, price, and many other factors will all be considered by a consumer in deciding whether he will or will not purchase a particular product. No two persons are identical in what they see or do, and being familiar with some of the basic processes of perception will help the salesman to relate more effectively with the customer.

Consumer attitudes

An attitude may be loosely defined as a person's state of mind, feeling, or disposition toward something. Such terms as belief, feeling, opinion, inclination, and bias are often used synonymously with attitude. Attitudes are also formed by a person's personal experiences in life, influences exerted by others, and the particular environment in which he lives. Consumers are not born with a given set of attitudes, for they are developed and formed as one lives.

Attitudes have a tendency to persist because of past experiences, agreement or harmony associations, and relating one factor with another. An illustration of conditioning by past experience would be when a man responds unfavorably to purchasing a new shirt made of a new synthetic fiber because he was dissatisfied with one previously purchased. This can happen even if the new synthetic fiber has been improved and is superior to the earlier one. Associations that are in agreement or harmony take place when the consumer responds favorably to a particular salesman because he (the salesman) is in agreement with the consumer's attitude. For example, if the consumer prefers conservative clothes and the salesman also has conservative tastes, the consumer is more likely to respond favorably to the salesman. An example of the effect of relating one factor with another is a situation where the customer judges the whole store and all its merchandise on the basis of a single unpleasant experience with a salesclerk.

Factors causing attitudes to change are contradictory influences, strength or intensity of the experience, multiple syndrome of circumstances, and emphasis of a particular factor. An example of an attitude changing because of contradictory influences is when a very thrifty and conservative bachelor buys an expensive, flashy car because his girlfriend liked it and he wishes to impress her.

The strength or intensity of an experience can cause an attitude to change. An illustration of this is when a person who is completely indifferent to the dangers of smoking suddenly changes his mind because of a heart attack.

Or the consumer may have an attitude unfavorable to the purchase of a particular product but reverses his attitude and makes such a purchase because of a multiple syndrome of circumstances. The circumstances may be that the product catches his eye, a friend strongly recommends it, almost everyone is currently using it, and he is influenced by a highly persuasive salesman.

Changes in an attitude can also occur when there is emphasis of a particular factor or when the consumer makes a decision to purchase on the basis of a single dominant factor which is stronger than several others combined. For example, a person may have definite attitudes regarding the brand name, color, material, and price he wishes to pay for a sport jacket but chooses one almost entirely on the basis of its style because of the attention it will attract. A change in the product or service, new ways of perceiving the product, a change in the type and/or amount of information available on the product, a change in how the product idea is communicated, and a change in the importance of the product are additional factors which can influence and change consumer attitudes.

Learning

Another important dimension of consumer behavior is learning. There are varying definitions, but generally the essence of learning is that it involves a change in a person's response or behavior. Human responses can either be learned or unlearned. Examples of unlearned responses are breathing, blinking your eyes, and crying. All other responses not based on instinct or reflexes are learned. Forgetting, which is the loss or fading of a thought that was previously in the mind, is another aspect of learning. And because of forgetting, it is often necessary for the salesman to repeat or reinforce an idea if he is to be effective

in influencing the consumer to buy a particular product or service.

Although learning takes place in different ways, the three basic processes involved are *stimulus*, *response*, and *reinforcement*. In order for a stimulus to take place, an object generally must be perceived, and motivation must also be present. The object may be physical or nontangible. For example, the customer may be stimulated by such physical things as a particular product, a given size or quantity, its color, or its style. Or in other cases he might be stimulated by such intangibles as the service he receives or the prestige value of the product. In addition to perceiving the object, the customer will also be motivated by love, security, safety, or many other motives.

The response is an action or reaction resulting from the stimulus and can be either physical or mental. Responses vary in speed, frequency, and/or in the nature of the response. Research has also shown that learning tends to increase as the speed, the frequency of correct responses, and the reward of the response increases.

Reinforcement is the third basic factor in the learning process. Definitions vary among authors, but it may be loosely defined as a condition which increases the probability of an identical or favored response. It can also be defined as a rewarding or satisfying situation which helps to stimulate the same response. There are three laws of reinforcement—the law of *effect*, the law of *exercise*, and the law of *readiness*. The law of effect refers to repetition of a satisfactory response. If an association is formed between a stimulus (a product advertisement), a response (going to the store to buy it), and reinforcement (experiencing satisfaction with the product), the connection of these three processes is generally strengthened by repetition.

The law of exercise relates to a form of conditioning. If the customer experiences the same stimulus a second time, he responds more quickly and with less difficulty because of his satisfying experience in the first instance. It is similar to a runner who continues to improve his performance as he continues to exercise and practice.

The law of readiness refers to the customer's ability and willingness to solve a problem. If he has the ability and willingness to learn, effective learning generally can take place. And conversely, if these two qualities are absent, then little or no learning will occur.

As previously mentioned, learning is any change in a person's response or behavior. Applying it to selling, then, means that the salesman must be able to change customers from negative or indifferent positions to positive ones if he is to be successful in making sales.

Dyadic interaction

There has been considerable research on qualities necessary for success in selling and on consumer behavior. However, most of these studies have been made exclusive of each other, and only in recent years has there been research on the interaction between the customer and the salesman. Such research is referred to as "dyadic interaction" where two separate units are treated as one. It is an integrated analysis of the roles played by both parties in a sale. These studies also focus attention on the transaction itself and on such factors as content of the transaction, average length of the transaction, and when and where the transaction takes place.

Other related variables also are isolated, controlled, and studied. Some of these studies have shown that the more alike the customer and salesman are in such factors as age and economic and social background, the greater is the probability for a sale. Other studies have indicated that dependent persons tend to favor more assistance from the salesman in arriving at purchase decisions, while independent persons tend to prefer a minimum of assistance. Insofar as the sex of the purchaser is concerned, some of these studies have shown that males are more likely to respond favorably to aggressive salesmen than are females. Research of this kind is relatively new, and the findings should not be accepted as hard-and-fast conclusions which will always apply. However, such studies emphasize the many variables that must be analyzed in order to better understand the interactions between the customer and the salesman.

True or false?

_____ 1. If two persons witness the same robbery of a bank, they are both likely to give identical accounts of the event.

_____ 2. A "straight" college professor may buy mod clothes because of a multiple syndrone of circumstances.

_____ 3. The three basic factors in the learning process are stimulus, response, and readiness.

_____ 4. Dyadic interaction research has produced some hard-and-fast conclusions regarding the interaction between the customer and the salesman.

Now turn to Answer Frame 3[4] on page 24 to check your answers.

chapter 5

INFORMATION ON THE COMPANY, THE PRODUCT, COMPETITION, AND ADVERTISING

Frame 1[5]

"An ounce of prevention is worth a pound of cure" and how carefully a salesman prepares for a sale will greatly determine how successful he will be. It is, therefore, important for the salesman to know certain things about his company, his product, his competition, and current advertising before approaching the prospective buyer.

Company information

The salesman serves as a personal representative of his company and should be well informed about its history, growth, and development. How has it grown since its beginning? What are its particular policies which distinguish it from its competitors? What is its present size and sales volume? What is the present price of its stock? What new product lines and improvements have been made, and what are its future plans and objectives? What are its attitudes and practices relating to current social issues such as pollution and civil rights? The salesman should also be familiar with central and regional operations of the company, where they are located, plus the names of major executives and some background information on each of them. More importantly, the salesman should know the company's policies and procedures as related to prices, discounts, delivery, credit, and service.

Product information

It is the salesman's responsibility to be well informed on his product. He should know how his product is made and be fully informed on its different styles, models, sizes, and prices. Markets are constantly changing and most products are periodically redesigned and improved; keeping up to date on product knowledge is, therefore, a never-ending process. The sources for obtaining current information on his product are many. They include company manuals and brochures, training programs, advertisements, magazine and newspaper articles, discussions with other salesmen, trade and association reports, and other related sources.

A salesman should also know the major selling points and disadvantages of his product or service and specifically how it differs from other products or services. For instance, how can it fulfill varying needs and problems of prospective buyers and what are its limitations? Every product or service has some limitations, and the salesman should know what they are and be prepared to clear up common misunderstandings and answer objections. Furthermore, the salesman should be informed on current product research and advertising. Such material can be shown and/or distributed to prospective buyers and serves as an

Answer frame 3⁴

1. False. No two persons are likely to perceive the same stimulus in exactly the same way. Two witnesses to the same event often tell vastly different stories based on different perceptions.
2. True. The clothes may have caught his eye, a friend (or his wife) may have recommended them, almost everyone else at the university was wearing them, and he was influenced by a highly persuasive salesman.
3. False. They are stimulus, response, and *reinforcement*. Readiness is one of the three laws of reinforcement.
4. False. The findings should be regarded as tentative at best, but relevant variables are being identified and future research is likely to produce more useful knowledge.

If you missed any of the above, reread Frame 3⁴ before beginning Chapter 5 on page 23.

Frame 1⁵ continued

effective tool for selling. In addition, the salesman should know about operating and servicing his product, as well as the guarantees and warranties that are offered.

Information on competition

Being informed about his own company and product is not enough; the salesman must also be well informed about the products or services offered by his competitors. Prospective buyers will frequently refer to competitors' products or ask specific questions about them. The salesman should, therefore, know the advantages and drawbacks of each competitive product and be prepared to explain and prove the particular merits of his product in comparison with specific competitor products. Furthermore, he should have some idea about the sales volume and market share of each competitor and know their basic policies and procedures as related to prices, discounts, credit, and service. Rather than directly criticizing the products of his competitors, the salesman should emphasize the advantages of his own product.

Advertising and selling

Advertising is addressed to the masses, while personal salesmanship is geared to specific individuals. Advertising is also designed to presell the product or service, and personal salesmanship is used to follow up with more detailed information and to close the sale. Effective advertising and personal salesmanship work together to achieve the same objective—namely, to stimulate sales. Each is important, and these two functions must operate together as a coordinated effort.

It is the salesman's responsibility to keep abreast of all current advertising conducted by his company. He must know the content of each ad and when it appeared. He should be able to explain to dealers the uses and advantages of advertising and show them how it can help them move the product off their shelves after he has sold it to them. The following are some common points he can mention: (1) advertising increases demand for the product or service. A dealer can sell advertised products more quickly than unadvertised ones because the consumer is presold to a certain extent and is already aware and informed about the product; (2) advertising creates faster turnover of inventories, and faster turnover means lower operating expenses and greater profits; (3) through advertising and branding, consumers can identify quality products that they wish to buy again. Such identification also helps to establish a good reputation for the dealer who handles the product; (4) advertising not only helps the customer to identify products, but also provides him with valuable information about their quality and performance.

Advertising also helps the salesman in many ways:

1. It develops customer interest and helps to presell products and services.
2. The salesman can use advertising to emphasize and reinforce sales points he mentions in his presentations.

3. Advertising reaches the masses and serves as a means for securing new leads and contacts. Thus, it often reaches some people whom the salesman, because of distance or other circumstances, is unable to contact.
4. Sometimes the salesman is unable to call on all his customers as often as he would like, and advertising helps him sell between calls.
5. The presentation of new ideas and information through advertising stimulates interest and increases motivation in the salesman himself.

To use company advertising effectively, the salesman should carry copies of current advertisements to show to prospective buyers. He should also be well informed on his company's total advertising program and be able to explain its uses and benefits to the buyer. Sometimes a buyer will ask questions on how he can tie his efforts in more effectively with the advertising campaigns, and the salesman should be able to give him appropriate suggestions. It is also the salesman's responsibility to get the buyer to use any direct-mail, point-of-purchase, or cooperative space advertising his company provides. Finally, he should obtain the buyer's reactions to, and suggestions concerning, his company's advertising in order to make it more effective.

It is recognized that the salesman's knowledge of his company, his product, competitive products, and current advertising will vary with his experience and training. It sometimes takes months and even years to prepare for a particular sales position. Furthermore, it is a continuing process, for markets and products are constantly changing. To keep abreast of these changes is an important responsibility of the salesman, which will greatly determine his success or failure.

Indicate whether each of the following statements is true or false by writing "T" or "F" in the space provided.

_____ 1. The salesman serves as a personal representative of the company and should be well informed about its history, growth, and development.

_____ 2. It is enough that a salesman thoroughly understands his company and its products in order to be successful.

_____ 3. Once a salesman learns all about his company's products, he can concentrate on other problems and not study his own products any further.

_____ 4. Advertising is an aid to the salesman, and he should carry copies of current advertisements to show to prospective buyers.

Now turn to Answer Frame 1⁵ on page 26 to check your responses.

Answer frame 1⁵

1. True. A salesman should know all about his company, especially its pricing policies, discounts, delivery, credit, and other services.
2. False. Being informed about his own company and products is not enough for a salesman. He must also be well informed about the products or services offered by competitors in order to discuss the relative advantages and disadvantages.
3. False. Most products are periodically changed and improved, and keeping up to date on product knowledge is a never-ending process.
4. True. Advertising helps the salesman by increasing demand for products, establishing a good company image, providing consumer information, reaching people the salesman cannot, and stimulating and motivating the salesman himself. The salesman should use these ads to support his presentation. The salesman should also provide feedback from the customer to make future ads more effective.

If you missed any of the above, you should restudy Frame 1⁵ before beginning Chapter 6 below.

chapter 6

CREDIT, PRICING, AND DISCOUNTS

Frame 1⁶

Credit and Collection

The three C's of credit. Many products or services are purchased on a credit basis, and the salesman should be familiar with the policies and procedures for granting it. Credit is permission to buy a product immediately and to pay for it later. Moreover, credit is a privilege, not a right, which means that the buyer is morally and legally responsible to pay for the products or services he receives.

In opening a personal credit account for the buyer the salesman must answer the following three questions: *Can the buyer pay* for what he purchases? *Will he pay?* What *amount of credit* should be given?

To answer these questions the salesman must have information about the buyer's capital, capacity, and character, commonly referred to as the "three C's of credit." Capital relates to the buyer's financial position. We need to have a picture of his assets, liabilities, and net worth. Capacity pertains to the buyer's weekly or monthly income. And character applies to the buyer's personal integrity, honesty, and past dependability in paying his bills. All three of these factors must be carefully analyzed in determining the buyer's ability and willingness to pay, as well as the amount of credit he will receive.

Sometimes a salesman will be so eager to sell that he minimizes the importance of credit. He may concentrate only on selling and look upon the collection of payments as management's responsibility. Such an attitude is harmful, because the salesman's cooperation is needed if the company is to operate a successful credit program. He should remember that profitable selling is measured, not by the number of units sold or their total dollar volume, but by the total amount of money actually collected as well as the expenses involved in collecting it. The salesman or personnel in the credit department should not be apologetic about asking for money owed to the company because it is only proper that a buyer should pay for the products or services he has purchased and used. If he doesn't, either the company or the salesman, or both, will suffer losses.

Why customers don't pay. Failure to pay for a product or service will vary from one customer to another. As Kirkpatrick points out, some of the common reasons are as follows:

1. The buyer does not understand or has been misinformed about the credit terms.
2. Sometimes the customer deliberately delays

making his payments because he is unhappy with the product.
3. Sometimes the amount owed is very small, and the customer prefers to postpone payment until the amount is larger.
4. Some customers are habitually slow in paying their bills, and several notices must be sent before they will pay.
5. Customers are sometimes careless or forgetful.
6. Occasionally a person will run short of money because of unexpected circumstances. Maybe he overbought, maybe he was in an accident, or maybe he had an unusual opportunity to buy something else.
7. A change in economic conditions or a sudden decrease in earning power can sometimes be the cause for delinquent payments.
8. Finally, there is a small percentage of people who are simply dishonest and deliberately avoid paying their bills.[1]

The policies and procedures for correcting these problems will vary from one company to another, and the salesman should be thoroughly familiar with them.

---

[1] Adapted from C. A. Kirkpatrick, *Salesmanship* (4th ed.; Cincinnati, Ohio: South-Western Publishing Co., 1966), pp. 417–18.

Indicate whether each of the following statements is true or false by writing "T" or "F" in the space provided.

    _____ 1. Buying on credit is a right guaranteed to every person.

    _____ 2. "Capital" relates to the buyer's financial position.

    _____ 3. A buyer's ability and willingness to pay, as well as the amount of credit he can receive are determined by using the "three C's of credit."

    _____ 4. Most customers who don't pay their bills are dishonest and do so deliberately.

Now turn to Answer Frame 1[6] on page 28 to check your responses.

Frame 2[6]

Pricing

Price Definitions. There are many different ways in which the word *price* is used, and the salesman should be familiar with them if he is to serve the customer in an effective manner. Following are some of the terms[2] commonly used:

List price. This is a quoted or published price from which buyers are normally allowed discounts.

---

[2] This listing of terms follows that given in Carlton A. Pederson and Milburn D. Wright, *Salesmanship: Principles and Methods* (5th ed.; Homewood, Ill.: Richard D. Irwin, Inc., 1971), pp. 198–201.

Answer frame 1⁶

1. False. Buying on credit is not a right but it is a privilege which creates a responsibility to pay for the product or service purchased.
2. True. It refers to the buyer's assets, liabilities, and net worth.
3. True. The "three C's of credit" do determine a buyer's ability and willingness to pay, as well as the amount he can receive. Capital (financial position), capacity (income), and character (the buyer's personal integrity, honesty, and dependability) are the "three C's of credit."
4. False. There are many reasons why customers may fail to pay their bills such as misinformation about credit terms, habitual slow payment, carelessness, unusual circumstances, changes in the economy, and so on. Only a small percentage of nonpayers are dishonest per se.

If you missed any of the above, you should restudy Frame 1⁶ before turning to Frame 2⁶ on page 27.

Frame 2⁶ continued

Net price. The net price is the final price after all discounts and allowances have been deducted.

Zone price. For some products, prices are equalized for certain zones or geographical areas. Many manufactured food products are priced in this manner.

Basing-point price. Under this system a price is determined from a given location or base point. There are both single and multiple basing-point systems. A single basing-point system is used when a manufacturer ships to buyers in different locations but charges all of them the same price regardless of the distance involved. A multiple basing-point system, on the other hand, is used when several production centers are used as basing points and charges are based on actual distances from each production center.

Postage-stamp delivered price. This pricing method is used when a company wishes to sell its product or service at the same identical price throughout its entire market.

Fair-trade price. This is a price established by contract between a manufacturer of a branded product and a wholesaler or retailer. The manufacturer decides what the minimum price will be and the wholesaler or retailer may not sell below this established price.

Guaranteed price. When prices are falling, buyers may ask the seller for protection against any further price decreases that might occur prior to the time the product is either used or resold to the ultimate consumer.

F.o.b. price. This abbreviation means "free on board" a railroad car, a ship, a plane, or a motor truck. Under this system the seller assumes the transportation charges to a given shipping point, and the buyer incurs the costs beyond that point. If the term *f.o.b. destination* is used, it means that the seller incurs the transportation charges from the seller's place of business to the final destination point.

F.a.s. price. This abbreviation means "free alongside" and is used on overseas shipments. The seller agrees to pay the transportation charges for getting the goods within reach of the loading cranes, and at this point title passes to the buyer.

C.i.f. price. This term means "cost, insurance, and freight" and is used in export selling. It includes cost of the goods, transportation costs to the seaport, charges for ocean shipping and insurance, and other charges for landing goods at a foreign port. Title passes to the buyer when the seller delivers the goods to the common carrier.

Is each of the following true or false?

_____ 1. Under a single basing-point price system all buyers of a product would pay the same price (including freight).

——— 2. Postage-stamp delivered price means that all buyers of a product or service would pay the same price (including freight).

——— 3. On goods shipped f.o.b. destination the buyer would incur all the freight costs.

——— 4. On goods shipped f.o.b. shipping point the seller would incur all the freight costs.

Now turn to Answer Frame 2[6] on page 30 to check your answers.

Frame 3[6]

Major laws regulating prices and trade practices. The salesman should also be familiar with the following major laws.

Sherman Antitrust Act of 1890. The purpose of this act was to prevent monopolies and restraint of trade. Criminal penalties were provided for violators and aggrieved persons were entitled to recover three times the amount of losses suffered as a result of the violation.

Pure Food and Drug Act of 1906. This act made illegal the adulteration and misbranding of food and drugs. It was strengthened and extended to include cosmetics and therapeutic devices by the Food, Drug, and Cosmetics Act of 1938. Today, foods, drugs, devices, and cosmetics entering interstate commerce, as well as production operations, are inspected. Penalties for violators of the act include seizure of illegal goods, injunctions to restrain unlawful shipments, and criminal prosecution of those responsible for the violation. In like manner, the Meat Inspection Act, passed in 1907, empowered the federal government to inspect and certify processed meat.

Federal Trade Commission Act of 1914. This act established the Federal Trade Commission, which was given the power to investigate and to issue cease and desist orders. The act declared "unfair methods of competition" to be illegal. The FTC regulates a broad variety of business practices which may tend to hurt other businesses or consumers.

Clayton Act of 1914. The Sherman Antitrust Act of 1890 was weak and had to be reinforced by the Clayton Act. This act broadened the latitude of antitrust prosecution by defining practices as unlawful "where the effect may be to substantially lessen competition or tend to create a monopoly." In other words, the government no longer had to produce proof of actual monopoly or conspiracy. Four particular situations were singled out to make the law more specific. They were certain types of price discrimination, tying and exclusive agreements, intercorporate stockholdings, and interlocking directorates. These practices are not illegal per se, but only if they substantially lessen competition.

State fair-trade or resale price maintenance laws. These laws are aimed at excessive price cutting and legalize resale price maintenance contracts through which the manufacturer is able to set or control the price at which his product is sold by distributors. In 1931 California enacted the first of such laws. It proved ineffective because retailers who did not sign contracts undercut those who did. It was reinforced by an amendment incorporating a "nonsigner's clause," which made the law apply to nonsigners and signers alike. The California law and the nonsigner's clause were widely adopted by other states, so that by 1941 all but a handful of states had fair-trade laws. But by 1967 the laws were made inoperative or repealed by court decisions in all but 16 states.

Robinson-Patman Act of 1936. The primary purpose of this act was to protect small business by regulating price discrimination on products bought by retailers. It held that "It shall be unlawful . . . to discriminate in price between different purchasers of commodities of like grade and quality where the effect of such discrimination may be substantially to lessen competition or tend to create a monopoly, or to injure, destroy, or prevent competition."

Miller-Tydings Act of 1937. This act allowed manufacturers in interstate commerce to make

Answer frame 2⁶

1. True. The freight charge is the same for all buyers regardless of the point from which the goods were shipped.
2. True. This pricing method is used when a company wishes to sell its product or service at the same price throughout its entire market.
3. False. The seller incurs all the transportation charges on goods shipped f.o.b. destination.
4. False. Title passes to the buyer at the shipping point. Thus, he incurs the transportation costs beyond that point.

If you missed any of the above, you should review Frame 2⁶ before turning to Frame 3⁶ on page 29.

Frame 3⁶ continued

resale price maintenance contracts which stipulated what the minimum prices would be at the retail level. At first the law was thought to be binding on nonsigners, but in 1951 the U.S. Supreme Court ruled otherwise. In effect this made the act of little help to national distributors, who would have to secure signed agreements with thousands of retailers if they hoped to maintain prices. (See McGuire Amendment.)

Wheeler-Lea Act of 1938. This act amended the FTC Act of 1914 to give the Federal Trade Commission specific authority to proceed against not only unfair methods in competition but also unfair or deceptive practices, including false advertising.

Antimerger Act of 1950. The purpose of this act was to prevent the lessening of competition by making it more difficult for large companies to acquire other large or even medium-sized companies in their own or closely related markets.

The McGuire Amendment of 1952. This amendment to the FTC Act reestablished the legality of price maintenance agreements in interstate commerce and made it enforceable among nonsigning dealers if one in the state had signed such an agreement. It enables manufacturers to enforce both minimum and maximum prices under the resale price maintenance provisions.

Unfair trade practice laws. Many states have recognized the dangers of predatory price cutting and have passed laws prohibiting unfair trade practices. These laws will vary, but generally they prohibit price cutting below a specified level which usually is set at approximately 6 percent above the invoice price.

Fair Packaging and Labeling (Truth-in-Packaging) Act of 1966. This act attacks deceptive packaging as well as labeling that is misleading or insufficiently informative. It requires that the label state net contents of the package. It does not, however, provide for the standardization of weights and measures in packages, something that needs to be done if the shopper is to be able to make quick comparison of values when shopping.

Consumer Credit Protection (Truth-in-Lending) Act of 1968. This act bans methods or stating credit terms that tend to hide the true annual rate of interest. It requires the lender to make clear the actual cost of credit by expressing it in writing in dollars and cents and showing it as a percentage figured as a simple annual rate on the amount borrowed, taking into account unpaid balances. Thus the borrower is now informed that what he might earlier have thought was, say, a 6 percent annual rate is really 18 percent on unpaid balances. The law does not establish maximum interest rates.

In addition to the above laws, many of the cities in the United States have regional Better Business Bureaus and local Chambers of Commerce. Although these organizations do not have the power to make actual arrests, they offer assistance to the consumer and businessmen by investigating complaints of fraud or unfair business practices reported to them and by establishing guidelines for ethical business practices.

Discounts

The salesman must also be familiar with discounts which will vary with the company and type of product or service being sold. Some of the common types are these:

Cash discount. The purpose of a cash discount is to encourage and reward early or prompt payment. A common cash discount is 2/10/net 30, which means that the buyer will be given a 2 percent discount if he pays his bill within 10 days from the date of invoice, and that otherwise the full amount must be paid within a 30-day period.

Trade or functional discount. Some companies sell their products to different types of distributors and will grant them trade discounts depending upon their trade classification and the services they perform. Trade discounts vary greatly, are quoted in series, and are related to the specific operating expenses of each trade. For example, a manufacturer of auto accessories may offer a 40 percent discount to wholesalers, 30 percent to dealers, and a 25 percent discount to chain stores.

Quantity discounts. There are savings in buying in large quantities, and this discount is designed to reward such purchases. They may be stated in a number of ways with typical bases being: (1) the number of total units purchased; (2) the dollar value of the order; (3) the size of the package ordered—which usually encourages sales that allow the seller to reship the merchandise in the original containers; (4)

bonus goods or "free deals," wherein the customer receives free merchandise or extra units depending upon the quantity ordered.

Advertising discounts. A schedule of advertising allowances may be granted to the buyer, depending upon the amount and type of merchandise he buys. However, advertising allowances are restricted by the Robinson-Patman Act, which prohibits the granting of such allowances unless they are offered on proportionately equal terms to all competitor buyers.

Early-order discounts. These discounts are designed to encourage the buyer to order early in the season.

Group discounts. These are discounts which are given to a group of buyers who pool or combine their purchases into a single order. The seller must also be able to justify such discounts on the basis of actual savings in selling to a group.

C.l and l.c.l. The abbreviation "c.l." means "carload"—that is, a full carload for which a higher discount is given. "L.c.l." means "less than carload," a shipment that carries a lower discount.

"Mixed car-lot" discounts. This is a common discount in the building material industry which allows the buyer to buy in smaller quantities rather than full car or truck lots of one product. Under this system, the buyer receives a balanced assortment of products and still receives a carload price.

There are many other types and forms of discounts, and it is the salesman's responsibility to know the ones that his company and his competitors offer.

Label each of the following statements as true or false.

_____ 1. The Sherman Antitrust Act of 1890 limits violators to civil penalties and the aggrieved person to recovery of the actual amount of loss suffered as a result of the violation.

_____ 2. The Clayton Act of 1914 was passed because the Sherman Antitrust Act was too weak.

_____ 3. Many laws directly affect the salesman and his freedom to quote prices and meet competition.

_____ 4. The purpose of cash discounts is to give better prices to select customers.

Now turn to Answer Frame 3[6] on page 34 to check your responses.

chapter 7

PROSPECTING

Frame 1[7]

Success in selling depends more and more on ability to find new prospects in the face of increasing competition. In most situations competition is too keen to allow a salesman the luxury of waiting for prospects to come to him. He must take the initiative, for sales do not just happen—they are the result of careful planning and hard work. Prospecting is one of the major means for increasing sales and earnings.

Of course, the amount of prospecting that must be done will vary with the product or service being sold. A retail salesman generally does little or no prospecting, as the prospect usually comes to the store in response to its advertising. In selling life insurance, however, the salesman usually must go into the field and locate prospects.

Considerations for selecting prospects

Not everyone is a good prospect, and the salesman has to be able to select those who are prospective buyers. We shall discuss some of the factors that aid selection in the following paragraphs.

The prospect should have a *definite need or want* for the product or service. Such a need can be specified by the prospect at the outset or may be an unrecognized one which the salesman creates or uncovers. In either case, a real need must exist or be developed, for selling a product to someone who doesn't need it is detrimental to both parties. Successful selling is dependent upon repeat sales, and repeat sales will follow only if the customer needs the product and is satisfied with it.

The prospect should have the *ability to pay* for the product or service. Sale of a product to someone who cannot pay for it is a disservice to the prospect, to the company, and to the salesman. In the case of the prospect, he will be forced to do without something else in order to pay for the product, or he will experience embarrassment and resentment when steps are taken to collect the money he owes. For the company, it can mean a loss from failure to collect the amount due. The salesman also suffers because selling to a person who is unable to pay may require considerable effort in trying to collect the money and may also reflect unfavorably on his judgment in selling to such a person.

The prospect should have the *authority to buy*. If the prospect has no power or authority to make the purchase, the salesman will often waste valuable time in contacting him. This does not mean, however, that the salesman should completely ignore someone who does not have the authority to buy. For example, an assistant to a purchasing agent may not have the authority to buy, but he may exercise considerable influence in helping the purchasing agent to make his decisions.

It is important that the salesman *be able to approach the prospect under favorable circumstances*. For example, the president of a large corporation would very likely not react favorably to a beginning salesman and might not even be willing to see him. Also, a prospect should not be approached at an inconvenient time or place, or when he is very busy and the salesman's appearance amounts to an annoying interruption. Care should, therefore, be exercised in approaching the prospect at a time and place that will be favorable to the sale. Needless to say, there will be some prospects who are always too busy to see the salesman. However, the salesman should generally respect the schedules and activities of his prospects.

Finally, the prospect should *be eligible to buy*. In some cases salesmen can sell only to wholesalers or retailers. It is obvious that in such instances he would be wasting his time if he were to select prospects who were ultimate consumers. Or in the case of a vacuum cleaner salesman, he should make his presentation to the mother who

is eligible to buy rather than to her teen-age daughter who may have nothing to say about the purchase.

Prospecting methods

As previously mentioned, prospecting methods will vary with the type of product or service being sold. Following are some of the methods which are commonly used.

The "cold-canvas" or "cold turkey" method. Under this method the salesman calls on any of the persons or companies within a certain class or group. He does not carefully preselect his prospects. Instead he goes from door-to-door and depends upon the law of averages to give him sales. It is sometimes a discouraging type of selling because many persons are not at home or in the office when the salesman calls without an appointment. This method of prospecting also has a high refusal rate.

Lists. To avoid the "hit-and-miss" results of cold canvassing, lists are sometimes used. These lists are carefully prepared with reference to sex, age, marital status, income, occupation, and so on, and help to identify those persons who might be interested in purchasing a particular product or service. Often these lists are purchased from commercial companies. They are frequently used for direct-mail advertising with the salesman following up on the inquiries received.

Company leads. Often prospective buyers will contact the company directly, and such information is given to the salesman who follows up on the call. Or managers of auto and appliance agencies will usually instruct service and repair personnel to inform the salesman of any persons who have older cars or appliances in need of repairs and are likely to qualify as prospective buyers.

Company advertising. Companies may receive inquiries from their advertising which are relayed to the salesmen. Sometimes a free gift is offered to the prospect who requests information about the product or service. Then a salesman delivers the gift and further explains the product.

Friends and acquaintances. Sometimes a salesman's friends and acquaintances will serve as a good beginning source of prospects. Also such

Answer frame 3⁶

1. False. *Criminal* penalties are provided for violators. Also, aggrieved persons are entitled to recover *three times* the amount of losses resulting from the violation.
2. True. Under the Clayton Act the government no longer had to prove actual monopoly or conspiracy. If "the effect may be to substantially lessen competition or tend to create a monopoly" the government could successfully prosecute.
3. True. Salesmen should be especially aware of the provisions of the Clayton Act, state fair-trade laws, the Robinson-Patman Act, the Wheeler-Lea Act, and the unfair trade practice laws. Those who deal in items sold on credit terms should understand fully the Truth-in-Lending Act of 1968.
4. False. Cash discounts are used to encourage and reward early payment of bills. A common discount is 2/10/net 30, which means the buyer will be given a 2 percent discount if he pays within 10 days from the date of the invoice, otherwise the full amount must be paid within 30 days.

If you missed any of the above, you should restudy Frame 3⁶ before beginning Chapter 7 on page 32.

Frame 1⁷ continued

persons as neighbors, relatives, fraternity brothers, business associates, people from whom the salesman buys, and others are excellent sources for locating other prospects.

The customer reference method. Under this method the salesman attempts to obtain the names of additional prospects from persons he has interviewed or who have purchased from him. With others helping him, this simple method can provide the salesman with a continuous supply of prospects.

The testimonial method. This method is similar to the customer reference method. It differs, however, by selecting persons who are well known and/or influential in the community. The salesman keeps in close contact with these people and uses their names and assistance in selling to others.

Group prospecting. Sometimes the salesman can make arrangements to give a group demonstration to clubs or service organizations. Or he can give demonstrations at the home of someone who is willing to sponsor him. Such products as cosmetics and household supplies are often sold in this manner, and the sponsoring party is usually rewarded with merchandise based on the number of persons who attend or the volume of sales made.

Surveys by junior salesmen. Some companies use junior salesmen to make surveys or canvasses

of consumer demand. They seldom attempt to sell the product but instead pave the way for the experienced salesman to make the actual presentation.

Sales spotters. These are persons who aid in prospecting by providing information on potential buyers. The associate receives cash or premium rewards from the salesman if this information results in a sale.

Public exhibitions and displays. Many companies display their product or service at public exhibitions. Products usually displayed at such shows are automobiles, boats, sporting goods and equipment, furniture, and many other products. Company representatives pass out literature and explain the product at these exhibits. They also secure the names and addresses of interested persons which are given to the salesmen.

Personal observation. The salesman frequently comes in contact with different people and different situations. If he is alert and keeps his eyes open, these circumstances can often help him to find persons who are likely to be good prospects.

In summary, there are many different methods for prospecting. Their use and effectiveness will vary with the product or service being sold, and the enterprising salesman will attempt to use as many as possible to increase his sales.

Indicate whether each of the following statements is true or false by writing "T" or "F" in the space provided.

_____ 1. Sales prospecting is the major means for increased earnings for many salesmen.

_____ 2. Everyone is a potential prospect for a sale and should be treated accordingly.

_____ 3. There is no one way of prospecting that is appropriate for all salesmen.

_____ 4. Group prospecting refers to the practice of groups of salesmen calling on people to persuade them to buy.

Now turn to Answer Frame 1⁷ on page 36 to check your responses.

Frame 2⁷

Additional considerations for effective prospecting

In addition to using the methods that have just been mentioned, the salesman should have an organized plan or system for identifying and evaluating prospects. He should establish a priority system for determining those that he will call on first, those he will call on second, and so on, and then arrange a schedule to carry out his program. He should also have goals or quotas for securing new prospects.

At the same time, he must be realistic in the quotas he sets. For if he spends too much time prospecting, he may not adequately serve the customers he already has and may consequently lose as many customers as he gains, or more.

Keeping good records and regularly following up on prospects is another aspect of good prospecting. It often requires several calls before a prospect finally becomes a customer. Therefore, the salesman should record what happened on each visit and plan each succeeding call to bring him closer to consummating a sale.

The salesman should also experiment with new methods and techniques—particularly if he has called on the prospect several times and has been unable to make a sale. Effective prospecting should result in sales; and if it doesn't, then the salesman should carefully reappraise his approaches and possibly consider other alternatives.

Last, but certainly not least, the salesman should always analyze his effectiveness in making a good impression or in creating a favorable attitude. Sometimes he seems to be using excellent methods and is working hard at it but has limited success. In such cases, it is often helpful to have another salesman or sales manager accompany him on some field calls in an effort to help determine the cause of the problem. On the other hand, a salesman should carefully examine a sale where he has been successful and see if the same methods will bring him success in comparable situations.

Guidelines for using the telephone

The telephone can be an important aid in prospecting and in increasing the productivity of the salesman. However, it should be used as a supplement to—not a substitute for—personal selling. It can be effectively used to make sales; to schedule appointments; to communicate new developments related to the product, prices, and promotion; to promote goodwill; to handle problems; to contact the home office; and for prospecting and preapproach work. Its many uses should not be overlooked, for it can save time, reduce travel costs, allow for more and faster contacts, enable the salesman to call on isolated accounts, and help to provide the customer with continuing service.

When using the telephone, the salesman should attempt to select prospects in accordance with some predetermined criteria. If possible, only those who have the potential for becoming customers should be called. The call should also be carefully planned and organized. Do not use the telephone for idle conversation and gossiping.

Answer frame 1[7]

1. True. The amount of prospecting varies with the product or service sold, but in some fields, such as life insurance, prospecting is the key to success.
2. False. Only those prospects who have a definite need should be sold. Further, only those who have an ability to pay should be considered. The prospect should also have authority to buy, he should be approachable, and be eligible to buy. Prospecting, therefore, is a narrowing-down process of finding customers.
3. True. Some salesmen are most successful calling door-to-door, others use commercially prepared lists. Company leads are also very effective, as are friends and acquaintances, referrals, and other such techniques. A salesman should try many of these techniques to see which ones work best for him.
4. False. Group prospecting involves giving demonstrations or talks to various clubs or organizations who are willing to listen. This technique has been very effective in selling cosmetics, household supplies, and other such goods.

If you missed any of the above, you should restudy Frame 1[7] before turning to Frame 2[7] on page 35.

Frame 2[7] continued

Instead, the salesman's objectives should be carefully determined, and the call should be designed to fulfill them. Nor should the telephone conversation be too long. Its primary use is to make appointments, to determine the prospect's general needs and wants, and to secure basic information.

At the beginning of the conversation, the salesman should identify himself and the company he represents and briefly explain the purpose of his call. Throughout the conversation the prospect's name should be mentioned when appropriate. More involved and detailed information should generally be presented by the salesman in person. It is helpful to keep brief notes on what has been discussed. An amazing amount of information can be covered over the telephone and the salesman sometimes is apt to forget some of the points that were mentioned.

It is also important for the salesman to remember that the buyer cannot see him. His voice and words are the only tools he has for developing a good impression, and the prospect will do some visualizing on the basis of what he hears. The salesman must, therefore, be familiar with basic techniques for effective speaking including speaking at a proper speed, using the right words and phrases, maintaining a satisfactory volume, and speaking in an organized and understandable manner. Furthermore the salesman must be a good listener and should learn how to detect through listening the various feelings of the buyer. It is also helpful to the salesman to have someone periodically listen to and comment on his telephone effectiveness. Sometimes the salesman can have an annoying manner which causes the listener to react negatively. He should, therefore, seek an evaluation from others in an attempt to improve his performance.

Finally, the salesman should remember that many buyers find it easier to say no to a salesman by telephone than they would in a face-to-face situation. For this reason, it is not wise to attempt to close most sales by telephone.

Direct-mail selling

Direct-mail selling can supplement personal selling activities. It can be used to secure direct orders, to obtain inquiries and solicit appointments, to invite prospects to the store or firm for a demonstration, to encourage customers to use the credit they have established, and to thank customers for their patronage. Some common forms of direct-mail advertising are sales letters, postcards, circulars, and inserts.

First, to be effective, direct-mail selling should be based on a prospect list which is current and up to date. The needs and status, as well as the mailing addresses, of consumers change, and a good list should accurately reflect the changes that have occurred from one period to another. Second, the direct-mail program should be carefully planned and organized. This includes consideration of details such as the appeal that will be used, the layout and appearance of the mailing piece, the timing of the mailing, the costs, and the total number of mailings. The third step is to acknowledge all inquiries immediately and to have a plan for determining which ones will be answered by a personal call, by telephone, by mail, or which ones will be delayed until additional information is received. Finally, every direct-mail program should be evaluated to determine the relationship of its costs to sales generated. Direct-mail selling can be an effective means for increasing sales, and its success is largely dependent upon how carefully it is planned and organized.

Label each of the following statements as true or false.

_____ 1. A salesman should give first priority to finding new prospects for his goods or services.

_____ 2. A salesman should experiment with new prospecting methods and new sales approaches.

_____ 3. Telephone prospecting is an excellent substitute for field selling.

_____ 4. The most effective direct-mail list is one which has been effective in the past.

Now turn to Answer Frame 2[7] on page 38 to check your answers.

Answer frame 2⁷

1. False. If a salesman spends too much time prospecting, he may not adequately serve the customers he already has. A salesman's first priority should be toward servicing his present customers.
2. True. If a salesman is not happy with the number of sales he makes to prospects, he should try new approaches to increase his effectiveness and keep his presentation fresh.
3. False. Phone prospecting is a supplement to, not a substitute for, personal selling. It can be effectively used to schedule appointments; to communicate new developments, prices, and promotion; to promote goodwill; and to handle problems. Any phone call should be carefully planned, with specific objectives, *before* the call is placed.
4. False. To be effective, direct-mail selling must be based on a prospect list that is current and up to date.

If you missed any of the above, you should reread Frame 2⁷ before beginning Chapter 8 below.

chapter 8

TYPES OF SALES PRESENTATIONS AND CONSIDERATIONS FOR EFFECTIVE DELIVERY

Frame 1⁸

Successful selling is based on presentations which are well organized and effectively delivered. Many things can go wrong during the course of a sales presentation, and advance planning is essential if the salesman is to achieve his objectives. Such planning and organization not only aids the salesman, but also saves time for both him and the buyer.

Types of sales presentations

There are three basic types of sales presentations. The first of these is the *standard memorized presentation* which covers specific selling points in a particular sequence and manner. Its advantages are that it insures that the complete and correct story will be told, provides the salesman with prepared answers to questions or objections that will be raised, and incorporates the techniques used by successful and experienced salesmen. This type of presentation also has inherent weaknesses, such as sometimes being too mechanical and artificial. Its structure often makes it difficult for the prospect to participate in the presentation, and it is also very embarrassing if the salesman forgets his place or lines. In addition, it cannot be used effectively if several products are being sold.

The second type of presentation is the *outlined presentation* which follows a basic outline but need not be memorized like the standard memorized presentation. Its key advantages are that it allows more give and take with prospects, it is more natural than the standard memorized presentation, and permits closer identification of the buyer's specific needs by giving him more opportunity to participate in the presentation. It is also more flexible and makes it easier for the salesman to get back on course if he is interrupted. Its drawbacks are that the salesman may wander and deviate from the basic selling plan and thereby fail to mention certain key points. Also, some salesmen may not be able to express themselves effectively when they speak extemporaneously.

The third type of sales presentation is the *program presentation*. It consists of a highly organized and comprehensive proposal written and illustrated after permission has been secured to make a thorough analysis or survey of the prospect's needs. This type of presentation is widely used in selling life insurance, industrial equipment, and other products and services which must be specifically tailored to the buyer. Its advantages are that it puts the emphasis on the specific needs of the buyer, it represents a more professional approach to selling, and it concentrates on proven absolutes, thereby avoiding often wasted time in exploring for the real needs and problems of the buyer. Its major limitations are that the salesmen may not be qualified to prepare a program. It is costly and time-consuming to prepare such programs, and some prospects may be reluctant or suspicious when such surveys are made.

It can be seen that each presentation has its respective advantages and disadvantages. Also, the type of presentation to be used will vary with the particular product or service being sold and the experience and training of the salesman. Generally, the standard memorized presentation is adaptable for single-line products where the ability and experience of the salesman is limited. The outlined presentation is more appropriate for multiple-product lines where a higher level of selling is required. And the program presentation is used for products and services which require a careful survey of the prospect's needs and problems.

Indicate whether each of the following statements is true or false by writing "T" or "F" in the space provided.

_____ 1. The standard memorized presentation should only be used by experienced salesmen where several product lines are being sold.

_____ 2. The outlined presentation is more flexible than is the standard memorized presentation.

_____ 3. The program presentation is more closely tailored to the customer's needs than are the other two presentations.

_____ 4. The program presentation is superior for all situations.

Now turn to Answer Frame 1⁸ on page 40 to check your responses.

Frame 2⁸ ———————————————————————————

Considerations for effective delivery

In addition to being well organized, the presentation must also be effectively delivered if it is to be successful. *What* you say and *how* you say it are of equal importance. Following are some points to help make the presentation more effective:

Answer frame 1[8]

1. False. It is most adaptable where the ability and experience of the salesman is limited and only one product line is being sold.
2. True. It follows a basic outline but need not be memorized. It reminds the salesman of points that should be made, but allows for more give and take with the customer.
3. True. This type of presentation involves a thorough survey of the prospect's needs and then shows him how these needs may be met.
4. False. Each presentation is designed for a given type of situation. But it can be disastrous to use the wrong type of presentation for a given situation (e.g. a memorized speech to sell insurance).

If you missed any of the above, you should restudy Frame 1[8] before turning to Frame 2[8] on page 39.

Frame 2[8] continued

Preparation.   Before he even begins the sale, the salesman should be well informed about his product or service and should also know as much as possible about the prospect. Each presentation in terms of content, organization, and pace should be specifically tailored to varying types of buyers. Some buyers are better informed or more critical than others. They differ on the basis of attitudes, income, educational levels, social status, and other factors. In regard to professional buyers, they often will have different policies or requirements relative to price, quality, and service. Whether he is selling to consumers or professional buyers, the salesman should recognize these latter differences and gear his presentation accordingly.

Organization.   The presentation should be effectively organized and some of the common patterns for discussing the product or service are:

a) According to the natural or sequential order in which the operations of the product or service normally occur.
b) By first mentioning the major points, then following up and filling in with the minor points.
c) By starting from the bottom and proceeding to the top, or from the front to the back, or from one side to the other side.
d) Or by organizing the presentation on the basis of a ranking of the prospect's buying motives.

Proper setting and showing.   The product should be displayed in a proper setting. A salesman selling a new car does not park it in a mud puddle in front of a dilapidated building. On the contrary, he displays the car in an attractive show window, and nearby there are comfortable areas where the buyer and salesman can privately confer. The product should also be realistically shown and handled. For example, in selling a tie the salesman should knot it and display it on a matching shirt or sport jacket. Proper lighting and comfortable surroundings are also important factors for effectively showing the product.

Show and demonstrate.   Actions speak louder than words, and an actual demonstration not only helps to convince the prospect, but also helps him to visualize what the salesman is talking about. Demonstrations can be used in selling insulation by having the prospect actually try to burn it in order to prove that it is fireproof; or in selling a radiator sealing compound by actually filling a leaking radiator to prove that the leak will stop. There are hundreds of instances where demonstrations can be used, and the salesman should utilize them whenever possible.

Outline key points.   When the salesman is explaining key points, he can be more convincing by also outlining these points on a small card or piece of paper. In this way, the prospect both hears and sees what the salesman is talking about. If a product has been lowered in price and the markdown represents a significant savings to the buyer, the salesman, in addition to explaining this point, could also illustrate it in the following manner:

Original price	$75.00
Markdown price	− 30.00
Savings	$45.00 or 60%

Such illustrating emphasizes the point and also helps the prospect to remember it.

Use of mnemonic words is also helpful in highlighting or outlining key points. For example, such benefits as *c*omfort, *a*ppearance, *p*erformance, *e*conomy and *s*ervice can be illustrated by the word CAPES.

Use charts, graphs, and illustrations. These visual aids should be used to reinforce explanations, for they facilitate understanding and help the prospect to remember. The old adage that a picture is worth a thousand words certainly applies to selling, and the salesman should use these aids wherever possible. Company advertisements and product training manuals serve as an excellent source for obtaining these materials. It is also relatively easy for the salesman to construct some of his own charts and graphs, for in many cases they involve nothing more than simple drawings or a listing of major points.

Appeal to a maximum number of senses. The salesman will always explain his product and service. He thereby automatically appeals to the prospect's sense of hearing. The senses of seeing, feeling, smelling, and tasting, however, are often neglected or overlooked. In selling pure Pennsylvania oil, the salesman can appeal to four of the five senses in the following ways:

Hearing—He explains the superior lubricating qualities of such an oil.

Seeing—He shows the prospect the rich green color of the Pennsylvania oil in comparison with the reddish tint which is characteristic of a lower quality oil.

Feeling—He lets the prospect rub a few drops of oil between his fingers. A pure Pennsylvania oil will be slippery, whereas a cheaper grade will have a more waxy feel.

Smelling—The pure Pennsylvania oil will have a strong and pungent smell, and the cheaper grade will be almost odorless.

Tasting—In the case of oil, it obviously is not appropriate for the prospect to taste it. However, with such products as food and beverages this is a highly effective appeal.

Is each of the following true or false?

_____ 1. *What* you say is far more important than *how* you say it.

_____ 2. There is more than one effective way to organize a presentation.

_____ 3. Actual demonstrations should be avoided because if they go wrong there is little, if any, chance for a sale.

_____ 4. You should appeal to only one of the prospect's senses to avoid confusing him.

Now turn to Answer Frame 2⁸ on page 42 to check your answers.

Frame 3⁸

Use the benefit-proof technique. The salesman will ordinarily mention the several benefits that his product or service will give the prospect. This is something almost all salesmen will automatically do, but the highly successful ones will go one step further. In addition to mentioning benefits, they follow up with respective proofs. For example, one salesman might say, "Our tire will give you longer mileage." But the one who follows the benefit with a proof will say, "Our tire will give you longer mileage because it is a steel-belted radial tire and track tests have shown that such radials give better results than fabric-belted tires. Here, let me actually show you the difference." Then he proceeds to show the prospect the difference between a steel-belted radial tire and a regular tire. All prospective buyers seek benefits—that is why they are interested in buying a particular product or service. However, despite their interests and needs, many do not buy because they are not convinced of the benefits the salesman mentions. To make the presentation convincing and relevant to the prospect, each major benefit should be supported with one or more proofs.

Answer frame 2[8]

1. False. They are of equal importance.
2. True. For instance, it can be organized according to the natural or sequential order in which the operations normally occur, by mentioning major points first, and so on.
3. False. Demonstrations are very effective and should be used whenever possible.
4. False. The more of his senses you can appeal to, the more likely the presentation is to be successful.

If you missed any of the above, you should review Frame 2[8] before turning to Frame 3[8] on page 41.

Frame 3[8] continued

Make comparisons. Comparisons emphasize differences and similarities, and the salesman should employ some of the following types.

SIMILES. A comparison can be made between qualities by using the words "like" or "as." For example, "Proper insulation is like wearing warm and comfortable clothing." Or, "This car consumes gas as a miser spends money."

METAPHORS. These are like similes, but the comparative word "as" or "like" is omitted. For example, "This car has the power of an elephant and the gliding comfort of a cloud."

ANALOGIES. These wordings take the prospect from the known to the unknown. For example, if a woman is reluctant to buy a power lawnmower because she feels it will be too dangerous to operate, the salesman might say, "Do you remember how frightened you were when you first began to drive? It is the same with operating a power lawnmower. You will no longer be afraid to operate it once you become accustomed to using it."

Listen and observe. A sales presentation is not a monologue, and the prospect should be encouraged to participate. Furthermore, you should not only listen to what the prospect says, but you should also observe the manner in which he says it. Does he speak softly or forcefully? Does he speak slowly or rapidly? Does he look away or directly at you? Does he reinforce his remarks with significant gestures? Does he speak in general terms or does he back up his comments with facts and figures? All of these actions and others should be carefully noted by the salesman, for they can serve as important clues in determining how to structure the presentation.

Use language and terms that the prospect understands. The language and terms used in the presentation should be geared to the particular prospect. Any terms or processes that the prospect might not understand, particularly when selling a product or service which is new or highly technical, should be carefully explained by the salesman. The prospect must first understand what the salesman is talking about before he can make up his mind to purchase it. In this sense, the salesman should regard himself as a teacher who must carefully explain the "whys" and "hows" of the product or service he is selling.

Emphasize key words. Certain words can also help stimulate favorable responses from the prospect. This idea can be illustrated in the following statement: "Our service is used by people who become successful and advance to responsible positions." The key or emotionally packed words in this statement are *successful* and *responsible positions* because they refer to the goals of almost every executive. Or when the utensil salesman says to the newlywed, "Just think how much easier it would have been for your mother if she could have purchased such utensils." In this instance the key word is *mother*, a word which generally has favorable connotations and powerful emotional values.

Use specific explanations rather than general ones. If it is an economical purchase, be specific and explain how economical it is in actual dollars and cents. For example, instead of saying that the product is "ecomomically priced," the salesman can be more specific by saying, "This chain saw was originally priced at $179.95 and has been marked down to $134.95, which represents a 25 percent markdown and a savings of $45.00." General terms to be avoided are *beautiful, better, excellent quality, comfortable, stylish,* and other similar terms. To make the presentation more interesting and convincing, more specific explanations should be substituted for these general and often overworked terms.

Be enthusiastic and confident. It is important that the salesman maintain his enthusiasm and confidence. It is difficult, if not impossible, for the salesman to make the prospect enthusiastic about his product and confident about what he is saying if he himself does not feel this way. Let your feelings show you believe in your product and are even excited about it. Enthusiasm is usually catching, and it also helps to maintain the buyer's interest in the product.

Vary the presentation. As previously mentioned, the presentation should be designed to fit varying types of buyers. At the same time, to help maintain the prospect's interest, the salesman should vary the speed and volume of his voice. The organizational pattern, particularly with lengthy presentations, should also be varied to avoid making the presentation too mechanical and boring.

Avoid distracting mannerisms and poor appearance. Such mannerisms as long and nervous pauses, needless fidgeting, hands in your pockets, slumping in a chair, sitting on a desk, rattling coins, swinging a chain, smoking, and so on, are usually very distracting and annoying to a prospect. The salesman should also be clean and properly attired in order to create a favorable impression.

Eye contact. It is difficult for the salesman to instill confidence in the buyer if he nervously looks away or down at the ground. Hence, you should look at the prospect while you are talking. This does not mean staring the prospect down, for this is just as bad as looking away. However, looking at him in a reasonably steady manner with occasional glances at the product or other related objects is the correct way to maintain good eye contact. In addition to keeping his attention, good eye contact also helps the salesman to better observe the buyer's reactions.

Control. The salesman should solicit responses from the buyer and also try to involve him in various aspects of the presentation. However, it is important for the salesman to maintain control throughout the presentation if he is to achieve his objectives. Too often a salesman can become sidetracked by a dominating prospect; and when this happens, the prospect usually succeeds in convincing the salesman that he (the prospect) cannot be sold.

Repeat and review. The salesman should periodically repeat and review to make certain the prospect understands and agrees with him. The salesman should not falsely assume that if the prospect says nothing, he automatically believes and agrees with everything the salesman has said. On the contrary, the prospect may be quietly seething inside, or worse yet, he may not even be listening. Consequently, the salesman should periodically pause to ask questions in order to determine if the prospect really understands and agrees with the points he has mentioned. Generally, it is also good procedure to secure agreement on one point before proceeding to another.

True or false?

_____ 1. The highly-successful salesman usually mentions benefits while other salesmen do not.

_____ 2. The salesman should actually encourage the prospect to participate in the presentation.

_____ 3. Good advice to a new salesman would be to use language the prospect understands, emphasize key words, use specific examples, be enthusiastic, vary the presentation, avoid distracting mannerisms, and maintain good eye contact during the presentation.

_____ 4. Two dangers in selling are that the prospect may say too little or too much.

Now turn to Answer Frame 3[8] on page 44 to check your answers.

Answer frame 3[8]

1. False. Almost all salesmen automatically mention benefits, but highly-successful salesmen follow this up with one or more proofs supporting each of the benefits mentioned.
2. True. The prospect's reactions during the presentation are important clues as to how to proceed. Thus, he should be encouraged to participate.
3. True. All of the points mentioned can aid in making the presentation more effective.
4. True. If the prospect says too little he may not be listening or he may be seething inside. If he says too much he may take control of the presentation and convince the salesman that he (the prospect) cannot be sold.

If you missed any of the above, you should restudy Frame 3[8] before beginning Chapter 9.

chapter 9

OPENING THE SALES INTERVIEW

Frame 1[9]

Objectives of the opening

There is an old saying, "Well begun is half done." The opening sets the stage for the remainder of the interview and greatly determines whether the salesman will succeed or fail. Within a very short time the salesman must make the prospect like him, determine the prospect's needs and problems, and determine and organize the approaches he will use for the remainder of the sale. This is no simple task, and its successful execution requires a great deal of alertness and skill on the part of the salesman.

In accomplishing these objectives, the salesman should be on time for the interview and should also be dressed in appropriate attire. He should approach the prospect with a friendly smile and handshake and introduce himself with a statement such as the following: "Good morning, Mr. Smith, I'm John Doe from the Central Equipment Corporation. You recently requested some information on our new conveyor belt, and I'm here to explain how it operates and how it can increase your profits. I appreciate this opportunity to talk with you. I know your time is limited, so I will be as brief as possible. I would like to begin by asking you some questions about your present operation . . .," and so on.

Note that the salesman has accomplished the following things in using this approach:

He has started off on the right foot by being on time and being properly attired.

He has established good rapport by smiling and introducing himself.

He mentions the prospect's name and also mentions it before his own name.

He identifies the name of his company.

He explains the purpose of his visit.

He expresses appreciation for the prospect's time and promises to be brief.

He begins by asking some basic questions in order to identify the prospect's needs and problems.

In short, he begins by being friendly and continues by being well organized and businesslike. If executed properly, such an approach will help to make the prospect like and respect him. It also puts the emphasis on the buyer's needs, because the salesman asks for basic information on the prospect's present operation. However, the salesman should learn as much as possible about the prospect's operation before calling on him. He should also listen very carefully to what the prospect tells him; and at the same time, he should determine the organization and approaches he will use in the remainder of the presentation.

The salesman's attitude and approach

In opening the sale, the salesman should be calm, relaxed, and "optimistically confident." He should realize how important the opening is, for first impressions are often lasting impressions. A poor start makes it difficult to finish well. The opening also takes very little time, but what is accomplished during this period will largely determine the final outcome of the presentation.

Some salesmen are ineffective because they feel they are bothering the prospect, particularly if the prospect is busy at the time they call. This definitely is not the attitude to have, for if the salesman feels this way, he will be handicapped at the start. If the prospect has a need for the product and it will help him to make or save money, the salesman should have no reluctance to approach him but should do so with confidence and enthusiasm.

There are many situations where a salesman will have little or no information about the prospect whom he encounters. For example, he may notice a new store being prepared for an opening and decide to call. Or a new buyer may have been assigned to an account which the salesman already services, and he learns of this change when he arrives. In such cases, he should not automatically assume that he must postpone his call until he learns more about the prospect; it is appropriate for him to call on the prospect immediately. A prolonged delay in order to learn more about the prospect may result in losing the opportunity for a new or continued account because of faster action taken by a competitor salesman.

Every salesman should also guard against assuming that once a sale is made, it is no longer necessary for him to learn more about the customer. On the contrary, successful selling is an ongoing process, and the salesman should continue to assemble information as long as he calls on the account.

Things to avoid

In executing the opening, the salesman should not resort to flattery or "honey-dripping" compliments in an effort to get the prospect to like him. If the prospect has done something which merits a compliment, then he should be complimented. Otherwise, such an approach should be avoided, because the prospect can easily detect insincerity.

Though the salesman should be confident and in control of the interview, he should be careful not to dominate it. Customers generally do not like "cocky" and overly aggressive salesmen. They usually resent being "pushed around," and the salesman who resorts to such high-pressure tactics will often only irritate and anger the prospect. Consequently, the salesman should encourage the prospect to participate in the interview, and he should be genuinely interested in securing the prospect's comments and reactions.

The salesman should not call on a prospect just for the sake of calling. There should be definite objectives for each call, and the salesman should strive to fulfill them. There is no excuse for taking up the prospect's valuable time when the salesman has no objective in mind.

Indicate whether each of the following statements is true or false by writing "T" or "F" in the space provided.

_____ 1. A salesman should begin preparing for a sales presentation long before he actually sees the prospect.

_____ 2. The opening sets the stage for the remainder of the interview and greatly determines whether the salesman will succeed or fail.

_____ 3. As a salesman, you should have the attitude that you are a problem solver and that you have something which will benefit the prospect.

_____ 4. An effective sales "opening" is to flatter the prospect so that he will like you.

Now turn to Answer Frame 1⁹ on page 48 to check your responses.

Frame 2⁹

Making appointments

Some salesmen feel very strongly that making appointments is necessary, while others feel it is too much bother. Normally, the advantages of making appointments are that they avoid the likelihood of seeing the buyer when he is busy and an appointment gives the buyer time to prepare for the interview. The drawbacks of appointments generally are that they often make it easy for the buyer to refuse to see the salesman and to put him off, and sometimes the weather or other circumstances will make it difficult to be on time or to keep an appointment. What use should be made of appointments is an individual decision which will vary with the product or service being sold and the particular circumstances of the sale. Therefore, the salesman should carefully study each sales situation and vary his approach according to the circumstances that prevail.

First-call obstacles

First calls usually are more difficult than subsequent calls because on an initial call the salesman may not have all the information about the prospect that he needs. He should, of course, learn as much about the prospect as he possibly can prior to calling on him. An attempt should be made to learn what product or service he is presently using; what his specific needs and problems might be; his major personality traits; his interests and community affiliations; his age, educational level, income, occupation, and other related information which might be helpful in determining how to approach him.

However, the salesman must realize that regardless of the information he has gathered about the prospect, he will often encounter certain obstacles on first calls. Many prospects have a fear of strangers which puts them on the defensive when a salesman first calls on them. They may not give the salesman a sufficient amount of time to tell the complete story about his product or service. Some prospects may state that they are too busy to talk with the salesman, and others may simply indicate that they have no need for or interest in the product the salesman is selling.

The salesman should expect such reactions from the prospect when he makes the initial call and be prepared to overcome them. To do this he must be skillful in analyzing people and establishing rapport. He must learn how to gain the prospect's confidence by being friendly and demonstrating a sincere desire to help him. He must learn how to secure and maintain the prospect's attention by relating the presentation to the prospect's specific needs and interests. And he must also know how to ask questions to which the prospect will respond. Experience will help the salesman to become more successful in overcoming these first-call obstacles; but more importantly, success in doing so requires careful analysis and training.

Label each of the following statements as true or false.

_____ 1. A salesman should dominate the interview and use high-pressure tactics if this seems necessary.

_____ 2. It is a good idea to call on a prospect occasionally just to say hello and maintain contact.

_____ 3. The first sales call is often the most difficult and requires special preparation.

_____ 4. Whether or not to make appointments is an individual decision which will vary with the product being sold and the particular circumstances that prevail.

Now turn to Answer Frame 2[9] on page 48 to check your answers.

chapter 10

HANDLING OBJECTIONS

Frame 1[10]

Common causes for objections

Customer objections are a normal part of the sales process. The salesman should expect them and be prepared to handle them. Objections will vary depending upon the particular buyer. Frequent underlying causes are:

1. The buyer lacks trust in the company or the salesman.
2. The buyer has a natural resistance to change in his purchasing habits.
3. The buyer does not have the required financial capacity to make the purchase.
4. The buyer does not need the product or service.
5. The buyer needs more information or fails to recognize his needs.
6. The buyer assigns a higher priority to the purchase of other products.

Knowing the causes for objections will help the salesman to do a better job in answering them. He should, therefore, carefully analyze the reasons behind objections before proceeding to answer them.

Common types of objections

Common objections can be classified further on the basis of price, product characteristics, the company or salesman, bad service experience, and use of procrastination to delay or avoid making a decision.

Price objections are expressed in such terms as:

Answer frame 1⁹

1. True. The salesman should learn as much as possible about the prospect's operation before calling on him.
2. True. Within a very short time, the salesman must make the prospect like him, determine the prospect's needs and problems, and decide upon and organize the approach he will use for the remainder of the sale.
3. True. If the prospect has a need for the product and it will help him to increase earnings, the salesman should be eager and enthusiastic in approaching him.
4. False. Only if the prospect has done something which merits a compliment should he be complimented. Such an approach generally should be avoided because a prospect can easily detect insincerity.

If you missed any of the above, you should restudy Frame 1⁹ before turning to Frame 2⁹ on page 46.

Answer frame 2⁹

1. False. Customers generally do not like "cocky" and overly aggressive salesmen, and the salesman who resorts to such tactics will often irritate and anger the prospect.
2. False. The salesman should never call on a prospect just for the sake of calling. There is no excuse for taking up the prospect's time when the salesman has no objective in mind.
3. True. An attempt should be made to determine what product the prospect is now using, what his problems might be, his personality and interests, and other such helpful information. Experience will help a salesman to become more successful in overcoming first-call obstacles.
4. True. Some salesmen feel very strongly about making appointments and others feel it is too much bother. There are advantages and disadvantages to making appointments; the salesman should carefully study each sales situation and determine whether an appointment would be opportune or not.

If you missed any of the above, you should reread Frame 2⁹ before turning to page 121 to work the First Review, which covers Chapters 1–9. Chapter 10 begins on page 47.

Frame 1¹⁰ continued

a) "The price is too high."
b) "I'm going to wait for a lower price."
c) "I don't wish to spend that much."

Product objections are often stated as:

a) "I don't like the style or design."
b) "I prefer a better quality."
c) "It's not appropriate for what I had in mind."

Company objections are characterized by comments such as:

a) "I don't like the business practices of your company."
b) "I prefer doing business with a company I know more about."
c) "I prefer trading with a smaller company."

Prospects may also often react negatively to certain *salesmen* because they have personality characteristics or do something which the prospect does not like. They may make the objections known in such candid comments as:

a) "I just can't trust you."
b) "I'd never buy from you because you're too high pressure."
c) "You just rub me the wrong way."

Objections based on *bad service experience* may be expressed in the following ways:

a) "You don't have a service representative in the immediate area."
b) "It takes too long to get service."

c) "You have a reputation for giving poor service."

Delay objections are mentioned in these terms:

a) "I wish to wait and look around a little more."
b) "I need more time to think it over."
c) "I would like to discuss it with someone else."

Considerations for handling objections

A positive attitude about objections will help the salesman to handle them better. He should welcome rather than fear objections, realizing that they are normal and that they will help him to establish better rapport with the prospect. Such an attitude takes the salesman off the defensive and gives him a greater degree of confidence.

The salesman can take the initiative in minimizing objections by providing information which answers them before they are mentioned. He can do this if he understands how buyers generally feel about a product or service and why they raise particular objections. The salesman should also know that the buyer will sometimes object simply because he wants to test the salesman or wishes to secure further information to help him to decide. Every product or service has its disadvantages, and the salesman should try to take the initiative in putting them in as favorable a light as possible before the buyer brings them up as objections.

All objections should be carefully analyzed, especially to determine if the buyer is close to buying but is deliberately delaying a decision by presenting superficial objections. In such cases, the salesman should know the prospect's priority of buying motives and gear his presentation accordingly. *What* he says and *how* he says it are of equal importance. It takes considerable skill, involving tact and precise timing, to be effective in answering objections. Moreover, the salesman should *reason* with the prospect rather than argue with him. A sales presentation is not a debate, and the salesman should answer objections from the buyer's point of view.

Before answering the objection, the salesman should make certain he thoroughly understands the buyer's reason or reasons for objecting. Sometimes the salesman is so intent on selling his product or service that he fails to listen to what the buyer is saying. Such an approach leaves the prospect unconvinced, and the objection will usually persist. Most objections are also raised or continue because the salesman has not given the prospect a convincing explanation. He should, therefore, attempt to prove all the benefits he mentions by:

Demonstrating his product, appealing to all of the prospect's senses—not just seeing and hearing but touching, tasting, and smelling as well.
Comparing his product with other products.
Appealing to the prospect's needs and wants, showing how his product will satisfy them.

The use of the following materials will also help the salesman to be more effective in handling objections: current advertising, charts, graphs, reference to guarantees and warranties, case histories, testimonials, current research reports, and so on.

Indicate whether each of the following statements is true or false by writing "T" or "F" in the space provided.

_____ 1. The greatest fear a salesman should have is a customer who raises lots of objections.

_____ 2. It is often very effective to debate with a prospect over various objections to establish your position.

_____ 3. A salesman would be wise to anticipate objections and have a ready answer for every one.

_____ 4. What you say in answering objections is more important than how you say it.

Now turn to Answer Frame 1[10] on page 50 to check your responses.

Answer frame 1[10]

1. False. Objections are a normal part of the sales process and should be welcomed rather than feared.
2. False. A salesman should *reason* with a prospect rather than argue with him. A sales presentation is not a debate, and the salesman should answer objections from the buyer's point of view.
3. False. The method used for handling objections varies with the type of prospect being sold. The way the objection is answered depends on the circumstances related to the sale.
4. False. What you say and how you say it are of equal importance. The salesman should be tactful.

If you missed any of the above, you should restudy Frame 1[10] before beginning Frame 2[10] below.

Frame 2[10]

Methods for answering objections

Recognizing that the method used for answering the objection will vary in accordance with the personality traits of the buyer and the particular type of objection that is raised, some of the commonly used techniques are outlined in the following paragraphs. Remember, too, that these methods may be used singly or in combination, depending upon the circumstances related to the sale.

Agree and qualify. This method answers the objection by first agreeing with the prospect, and then tactfully qualifying the answer or presenting additional information which offsets it. For example, the prospect may say, "I'm not interested in your product because I can buy it at a lower price from someone else." The salesman replies, "Yes, this is true. However, the competitive products are of much lower quality and will last half as long as ours. (The salesman should carefully explain and prove this statement.) Therefore, you are really paying less for our product." From a psychological standpoint this is a highly effective method because the salesman never directly disagrees with or contradicts the prospect.

Make the objection serve as a selling point. This method takes the very objection raised by the prospect and converts it into a selling point. For example, the prospect may say, "I don't care for this particular style because it currently is not being worn." The salesman replies, "That's absolutely correct and that's why I'm showing you this particular style. It's the newest design, which soon will be very popular, and you can be one of the first to wear it." Or the prospect might raise the following objection in connection with a new type of printing press. "I don't believe I'm interested in your press because to my knowledge no one in this area is using one." And the salesman might reply, "That's right, and that's exactly why I'm showing it to you. You have a bigger operation and are more progressive than the other printers in this area. Not only will it give you increased production and lower operating expenses, but it will also give you the opportunity to set a new standard in your area."

The effective use of this method is usually dependent upon the salesman's being well informed about the prospect's buying motives and being able to determine what he really wants. In using it, the salesman should also be very careful not to use high-pressure tactics or to offend the prospect.

Ask questions for further explanation. Sometimes the salesman may not understand the nature of the objection and must ask for more information before he can give an effective answer. For example, the prospect might raise the following objection about a new systems program. "Your system is probably O.K. for most companies, but it certainly won't work in mine." Before answering such an objection, the salesman will have to have the prospect explain what he presently is doing and also determine why he believes the proposed system will not work. Sometimes the objection is not a truly valid one, and the salesman can ask certain questions which will result in having the prospect answer his own objection. In buying a truck, the prospect may say, "I can buy a more stylish model from other dealers." And the salesman in a polite and courteous manner asks, "Is style your most important consideration for buying a truck or are you more interested in performance and economy of operation?" A common reply by the prospect might be, "I'd like to have all three, but I know this isn't possible, so I'm definitely more interested in its performance and economy."

Agree that the objection is valid. Sometimes the objection raised by the prospect is a legitimate one. In such cases the salesman should not be afraid to admit the objection, for no product or service is perfect in every respect. For example, the prospect may say, "I don't like an eight-cylinder car because it consumes more gas than a six-cylinder car." The salesman replies, "That's absolutely correct, but the eight-cylinder car also gives you more room, a more comfortable ride, and considerably more power." When the prospect mentions a valid objection, rather than dwelling on a futile discussion of its negative aspects, it is better for the salesman to quickly admit it and then to shift to a discussion of its positive aspects.

Delay the answer. Sometimes the prospect will raise an objection before the salesman has had an opportunity to explain his product or service. In such cases, the salesman can politely say, "That's a good point and with your permission I will answer it in a moment. But first it is necessary for me to explain how our product is made, and in so doing I know it will answer your question."

Politely deny that the objection is valid. The salesman will seldom directly contradict the prospect, and this method should be used only if necessary and supported by the facts. However, the prospect will sometimes be completely wrong, or he will stubbornly persist in raising an invalid objection. In such cases, the salesman should clearly and politely deny the objection. For example, the prospect may say, "I've been told that you sell this same product for 25 percent less in other areas." The salesman can reply, "Someone has either misinformed you or you are confusing our company with another one, for we sell our product at the same price to everyone and have never deviated from this policy." The salesman should speak in such a manner as to avoid antagonizing the prospect; and such an answer will usually be accepted. However, if the prospect still persists with such an objection, then the salesman should ask for the name of the party who purchased the product at a lower price, and when and where such a transaction took place. He should also attempt to check it out immediately and tell the prospect that he will call back within one or two days with a complete report.

Pass up or ignore the objection. Sometimes the prospect is not serious about the objection he raises or he mentions an objection which doesn't warrant a serious answer. For example, the prospect might facetiously say, "I understand that you also supply a maid with every vacuum cleaner you sell." The salesman might humorously reply, "We would like to, Sir, but unfortunately they're pretty hard to find these days."

Indicate whether each of the following statements is true or false by writing "T" or "F" in the space provided.

_____ 1. If a customer makes a valid objection, the salesman should agree with him and then offer an explanation.

_____ 2. Often an objection can be overcome by questioning the importance of the point.

_____ 3. Postponing the answer to an objection often gives a salesman a chance to explain his product further.

_____ 4. A salesman should never flatly deny an objection because it may irritate the prospect.

Now turn to Answer Frame 2¹⁰ on page 52 to check your responses.

Answer frame 2¹⁰

1. True. An effective technique for answering objections is to first agree with the prospect and then tactfully present information which offsets it.
2. True. Sometimes the objection is not a truly valid one, and the salesman may ask certain questions which will result in having the prospect answer his own objections.
3. True. Often the answer to an objection is contained in the sales presentation and may be brought up at the proper time if the prospect will agree.
4. False. In cases where the prospect is completely wrong, the salesman should clearly and politely deny the objection, and if the salesman speaks in a manner which does not antagonize the prospect, the answer will usually be accepted.

If you missed any of the above, you should restudy Frame 2¹⁰ before beginning Chapter 11 below.

chapter 11

CLOSING THE SALE

Frame 1¹¹

The close is the culminating stage of the sales process, the point at which the prospect decides whether or not he will buy. The salesman should, therefore, be well informed and skillful in executing the close.

Common difficulties in closing

The salesman sometimes "tightens up" when he reaches the close, and the buyer can consciously or unconsciously detect this pressure. When this happens, the success of the sale is greatly impaired, for if the salesman is to instill confidence in the buyer, he himself must be confident and in control of the sale. On the other hand, the salesman may try so hard to close the sale that he uses high-pressure tactics and causes

the buyer to become defensive. In either case—if the salesman is too nervous or tries too hard to make a close—the sale will be seriously jeopardized.

Inadequate preparation and faulty presentations also make it difficult for the salesman to close. If he has done a poor job of identifying the prospect's needs, or of showing him how his product or service fulfills these needs, his close will undoubtedly fail. A good close is dependent upon careful planning and effective execution of all stages of the sale process. In this sense, selling is comparable to a chain which is no stronger than its weakest link.

Successful closing also requires experience, constant analysis of closing attempts, and experimentation. Closing is an art which must be developed through practice. It is not developed overnight, and to be successful the salesman must constantly work at revising and improving his closing techniques.

Considerations for effective closing

Timing. Many successful salesmen believe that the best time to attempt to close a sale is when the buyer has indicated in some way he is ready to buy. When that moment will occur will vary greatly. One prospect can decide that he wants a particular product or service on the first call, or before the salesman has given his complete presentation. On the other hand, it may be necessary to approach another prospect several times, and each visit may require a very complete and lengthy presentation.

The proper time to close, therefore, depends upon the type of prospect being approached, the nature and extent of his needs (whether they are immediate or anticipated in the future, whether they are major or minor, and so on), and whether he has the financial capacity to buy. The salesman should recognize that each buyer is different and his close should be specifically geared to the personality and needs of the buyer at hand.

Also, the close should not be looked upon as a separate part of the sale which occurs at the end of the presentation. On the contrary, what is done at the very beginning of the sale will greatly determine the outcome of the close. It is related to all phases of the sales process and is built and developed as the sale progresses.

Closing signals. Prospects may signal that they are ready or are not ready to buy by their expressions, participation in the presentation, or their comments. If the buyer frowns or looks confused, he generally is not ready to buy. In such cases, the salesman must further explain the product and/or give more convincing proof that it will fulfill the prospect's needs.

The prospect's degree of involvement or participation in the presentation may also indicate his readiness to buy. For example, if a prospect tries on one particular sports jacket several times and looks at himself admiringly in the mirror, he is more ready to buy than the prospect who simply looks at the sports jacket and continues examining others. Or in buying an automobile, the prospect who examines everything very carefully, starts the engine, and asks to drive the car is usually more interested than the prospect who says or does nothing.

The most accurate closing signals, however, are furnished by the prospect's comments. What he says and the questions he asks are of cardinal importance in determining his readiness to buy. Seldom will he suddenly say, "I like it and want to buy, now just tell me how much it costs." His comments are usually less direct and obvious and are more apt to be expressed in the following ways:

"What would my monthly payments be?"
"How soon could you deliver this product to me?"
"How much would you allow on a trade-in?"
"It's more powerful and economical than my present boat motor, and I know my family would enjoy it, too."
"It's priced right and is also better than anything else I've seen."

Questions or comments such as these usually indicate that the prospect is genuinely interested in the product or service, and indirectly he may be telling the salesman that he wants to buy. Sometimes a salesman will become so engrossed in what he is talking about that he fails to look for or recognize common closing signals. Hence, he should carefully analyze the prospect's expressions, his participation in the presentation, and his comments in order to become more effective in closing the sale.

Frequency of trial closes. Very seldom will a sale be closed on the first try. More likely it will require further trial or attempted closes. These trial closes should also be varied, for to use the same method each time is often ineffective repetition which fails to bring the salesman closer to closing. A good principle to follow is to try to close as often as good judgment dictates, and in a manner that will not irritate or antagonize the prospect.

Opportunities for attempting a close may occur at the following times in the sales process:

At the beginning or early in the presentation.
After a demonstration which is geared to a major buying motive.

After a major objection has been satisfactorily answered.

After the prospect has given a series of "Yes" answers.

After the first complete presentation.

After second, third, or fourth follow-up presentations.

After several calls.[1]

Trial or preliminary closes. Inasmuch as more than one close is usually necessary to make a sale, the salesman will often use a trial, or preliminary, close which is designed to prepare the prospect for the final close and to determine what must be done to achieve it. Trial closes are usually necessary because:

The prospect is not completely ready for a final close.

There may be some questions about the prospect's priority of buying motives.

Additional information has to be presented or the prospect does not sufficiently understand the points that have been covered.

The salesman may have failed to answer the prospect's objections satisfactorily.

Consequently, the salesman should carefully plan the trial close and analyze it in terms of what has to be done to develop and execute a subsequent close.

Control of the sale. As previously mentioned, the salesman should control, but not dominate the sales interview. If the prospect takes over, closing attempts by the salesman become extremely difficult, if not impossible. The salesman should also be confident and determined, but at the same time avoid being "pushy" or using high pressure. In short, the salesman should encourage the prospect to participate in the presentation, but the salesman should always retain control.

Indicate whether each of the following statements is true or false by writing "T" or "F" in the space provided.

_____ 1. A salesman should not stop until he has given his complete sales presentation.

_____ 2. The only way a salesman can determine whether a prospect is ready to buy is to ask him directly.

_____ 3. Many times salesmen miss signals from the buyer which indicate that he wants to buy.

_____ 4. A salesman often must make several attempts before he can actually close a sale.

Now turn to Answer Frame 1[11] on page 56 to check your responses.

Frame 2[11]

Reserve selling points. The salesman should not exhaust all the selling points that apply to his product or service before attempting a close. This is generally poor practice, because if the close fails after the complete presentation, he has nothing more to offer. It is like a quarterback who plays so hard during the first half of the game that he is unable to finish the second half. The salesman

should keep some selling points in reserve to serve as ammunition for subsequent closes.

Fit the item and quantity to the prospect's needs. The salesman's chances for a successful close are greatly increased if what he is trying to sell is what the prospect wants and is in the quantity the prospect needs. If he suggests the wrong item or the right item in the wrong amounts, he will usually meet strong opposition, and his close will fail. The salesman should remember that successful selling is based not on getting the prospect's first order but on securing the prospect's

---

[1] This listing is based on Carlton A. Pederson and Milburn D. Wright, *Salesmanship: Principles and Methods* (15th ed.; Homewood, Ill.: Richard D. Irwin, Inc., 1971), Figure 14–1.

continued patronage. His objective should be a satisfied customer who makes repeat purchases rather than the immediate purchase alone. Such an attitude will help the salesman to sell the prospect only what he needs and in the proper amounts.

Methods for closing

There are many different methods for closing, and the methods chosen will depend upon the wants and personality of the buyer, the urgency of his needs, the number of closes that have been attempted, the number of times the prospect has been visited, and so on. Following are some of the common methods that are used.

The alternative-choice close. This close does not ask the prospect if he wishes to buy but assumes that he *wants to* and *is ready* to buy. This method is designed to ask an alternative question which results in a sale regardless of the prospect's choice rather than asking a question which can be answered with a no. For example, the salesman does not say,

"Do you wish to purchase this shirt?" Instead, he assumes that the prospect is ready to buy and gives him a choice by saying, "Do you wish to purchase the plain colored shirt or the striped one?"

Other examples are:

"Do you wish to pay cash or charge it?"
"Do you want us to deliver the product today or tomorrow?"
"Did you wish to purchase one dozen or two dozen?"

In using this method the salesman must be reasonably certain that the prospect wishes to buy; otherwise it will appear that he is using high-pressure tactics.

Securing a series of acceptances. This method of closing the sale is executed by asking the prospect a series of questions to which he will answer yes. In this way a receptive attitude is developed, and it helps pave the way for a favorable response to the major question(s) in the close. A clothing salesman may implement this method in the following manner:

Salesman: "Have you noticed how lightweight this jacket is?" (The salesman places the jacket in the prospect's hands.)

Prospect: "Yes, it is light. It's not much heavier than a shirt."

Salesman: "I'm also assuming that you want a jacket that is currently in style?"

Prospect: "Yes. I do."

Salesman: "Well, this is the latest style which is currently being worn on campus. Have you seen it recently?"

Prospect: "Yes, I saw several students wearing jackets like this at last week's football game."

Salesman: "We also realize that students have limited budgets and that price is very important to them. It was that way when I was in college and I'm sure it's the same today!"

Prospect: "It sure is!"

Salesman: "Well, we have an introductory sale offer this week and most of our merchandise is reduced by 20 percent."

Prospect: "Is there a reduced price on this jacket?"

Salesman: "Yes, but only for this week. Let's have you try it on to see how it fits."

Prospect: "It fits perfect."

Salesman: "Yes, it does. It also looks good on you. Should I wrap this one up, or do you wish to look at some of the others?"

Prospect: "No, this jacket is exactly what I've been looking for and I would like to charge it to my account."

The above example is greatly condensed, and in actual practice the movement from one question to another would be slower and less direct. It should also be noted that a no answer can be equivalent to a yes answer, as illustrated in the buyer's last statement.

Answer frame 1¹¹

1. False. The correct time to close a sale is when the buyer indicates he is ready to buy. Often a salesman need not make a complete presentation or *any* presentation if the prospect is ready and willing to buy.
2. False. Prospects may indicate that they are or are not ready to buy by their expressions, participation in the presentation, or their comments.
3. True. Sometimes a salesman will become so engrossed in what he is saying that he fails to look for or recognize common closing signals.
4. True. Very seldom will a sale be closed on the first try. More likely it will require two or more attempts.

If you missed any of the above, you should restudy Frame 1¹¹ before turning to Frame 2¹¹ on page 54.

Frame 2¹¹ continued

Label each of the following statements as true or false.

_____ 1. A salesman should make as many points as possible before attempting to close the sale.

_____ 2. Salesman should try to convince the prospect to buy the maximum number of items on the first call in case the prospect does not buy from him again.

_____ 3. A salesman should be careful in using "the alternative-choice close" with all buyers.

_____ 4. It is often effective to have the prospect answer a series of minor questions with "yes" answers so he is predisposed to answer "yes" to a major request to buy.

Now turn to Answer Frame 2¹¹ on page 58 to check your answers.

Frame 3¹¹

Summarize and review. It is good practice at the end of the presentation to summarize and review the major selling points of the product, particularly as they relate to the prospect's buying motives. Such a summary or review helps the prospect remember what had been covered and paves the way for the close. It also gives the salesman an opportunity to determine if there are any additional questions that must be answered. In selling a tire it might be used in the following manner:

"The tire I have shown you has two tough fiber glass belts backed up by two nylon cord plies for inner strength, is guaranteed for 36 months rather than 12 or 24 months, is reduced in price by 20 percent, and we will allow you $5 on each of your old tires."

Generally at the end of the summary the prospect will either indicate that he wishes to purchase the product or he will ask for additional information.

Get the prospect to make minor decisions first. The salesman should get the prospect to agree on minor points before going on to major considerations. For example, in selling life insurance the salesman might first get decisions as to the type of insurance the prospect wants and whom he would designate as his beneficiary. These are generally minor points which can be settled before proceeding to such major points as the face amount of the policy and the monthly premium costs. This method is closely related to "assuming the sale is made" and "securing a series of acceptances." It differs by drawing a distinction between major and minor points.

The conditional method. In using this

method, the salesman offers to do something if the prospect agrees to buy. For example, in selling cattle feed the salesman might say, "If I can show you that our feed will give you faster gain at a lower price, will you be interested in buying it?" This close can be used with buyers who have difficulty in deciding to buy. It should not be used, however, to cause a prospect to buy something which he does not want or need. Such selling would be high pressure and unethical. But if the prospect has a need for the product, and it will definitely benefit him, then the salesman is justified in using this approach.

Pointing out greater risks of waiting. Sometimes the prospect will delay purchasing a product simply because he cannot make up his mind and thinks he has nothing to lose by waiting. In such cases, the salesman can refer to higher costs or the creation of greater risks if the prospect waits. For example, in selling a file cabinet the salesman might inform the customer of the fact that, within ten days the same cabinet will cost approximately $5 more because of the new labor and steel prices which will go into effect at the end of the month. Or in selling insulation the salesman could say, "Next month will be much colder, and your heating bills will be even higher than they presently are. Furthermore, we now have time to do the work, but next month will be the peak of the season and we may not be able to schedule your job for several weeks." The salesman must be sincere and truthful in using this method. He must also be reasonably certain of what will happen in the future rather than basing his statements on rumor or conjecture.

True or false?

_____ 1. It is a good practice at the end of a sales presentation to summarize and review major selling points.

_____ 2. Agreement should normally be secured on minor sales points before proceeding to major or more critical points.

_____ 3. The conditional method of offering the prospect something if he agrees to buy should be used on those buyers who do not need the product.

_____ 4. If a prospect delays a purchase decision because he cannot make up his mind, it is a good idea to point out the possible cost of waiting.

Now turn to Answer Frame 3¹¹ on page 58 to check your answers.

Frame 4¹¹

Limited supply. This method is used for products which are selling very rapidly and where the supply is limited. For example, the real estate salesman may say, "You have indicated that this lot is ideal for your purposes, and inasmuch as it is the last piece of frontage on the lake, do you want me to reserve it for you now so you won't be disappointed?" Or in the case of selling ties, the salesman says, "There are only three left, and we won't be able to reorder this particular style again." In this instance, the close is a combination of pointing out a limited supply and the possibility of incurring greater risk by waiting. Again, this method should not be used in a false or insincere manner.

Special offer or concession. Implementation of this method should be handled with care, for sometimes it gives the prospect the impression that he will get a better offer if he deliberately delays his purchase. Some companies promote the sale of their product by offering such inducements as a free accessory, a discount from the regular price if a certain quantity is purchased, an introductory offer, and so on. Giving the prospect something "extra" or "something for nothing" often serves as an effective tool in influencing him to buy.

Alteration of product. Sometimes the prospect will refrain from buying the product because it is not exactly what he wanted. He may object

Answer frame 2¹¹

1. False. Making all the points of a sale before closing is generally a poor practice because, if the close fails, the salesman has nothing more to offer.
2. False. A salesman's chances for a successful close and a favorable long-term relationship with the customer are increased if he sells only the specific number of items wanted and needed by the customer.
3. True. In using the "alternative-choice close," the salesman must be reasonably certain that the prospect wishes to buy, or it will appear that the salesman is trying high-pressure tactics.
4. True. A series of "yes" answers to minor questions develops a receptive attitude in the prospect which paves the way for a favorable response to the major question(s) in the close.

If you missed any of the above, you should reread Frame 2¹¹ before turning to Frame 3¹¹ on page 56.

Answer frame 3¹¹

1. True. A summary or review helps the prospect remember what has been covered and paves the way for the close.
2. True. Once agreement has been reached with the prospect on minor selling points, it is easier to get agreement on major points which logically follow the initial agreements.
3. False. The conditional method can be used with buyers who have difficulty in deciding to buy, but it would be unethical to use such a technique on a buyer who does not need the good or service.
4. True. The technique of pointing out the cost of waiting should only be used when, in fact, costs are expected to rise and would adversely affect the prospect.

If you missed any of the above, you should restudy Frame 3¹¹ before turning to Frame 4¹¹ on page 57.

Frame 4¹¹ continued

to buying a picture frame because it is the wrong color. In such a case it might be possible for the salesman to repaint the frame in the color the prospect wishes. Or the prospect may wish to buy the same quantity, but because of convenience in handling he prefers it in several smaller containers rather than one large container. When the salesman offers to alter the product to the prospect's personal specifications, it is difficult for the prospect to refuse the offer. However, the salesman should always be certain the product can be altered, that the changes will be what the customer wants, and that the product can still be sold at a profit.

Trial offer. A trial offer can be highly effective in getting the prospect to buy. It is especially useful in those cases where the salesman has done everything he possibly can and his only remaining alternative is to let the prospect use the product on a trial basis. The trial may be for a few days or a few weeks; and at the end of this period, the salesman returns to attempt another close. The offer is particularly effective when there is no obligation on the part of the buyer, for it gives him a chance to determine for himself if the product will fulfill his needs. Sometimes the prospect fails to use the product. However, the salesman can greatly minimize this problem by calling the prospect to determine if he has any questions in the use and operation of it.

Bringing in help for the close. Sometimes the salesman needs assistance from another person to help close the sale. This is especially true for highly technical products or services. On the other hand, the second person may be able to explain something which the first salesman missed. This approach must be used with care, for sometimes the prospect views the appearance of a second party as a means to "gang up" and pressure him.

Changing the course of the interview. Occasionally, after several closes have been attempted, it becomes necessary for the salesman to switch gears. He must try another course. On doing so, he might suddenly stop talking about his product and switch the conversation to neutral ground. Or he may start to pack up his things and give the impression he is preparing to leave, thus reducing any tensions that may have developed and relaxing the prospect's buying defenses. Then, seeing the customer relaxed, he can casually refer to a point he failed to mention previously. If the prospect does not stop him, he will then enlarge on this point and eventually try another close. In using this method, the salesman must not repeat himself and should be very careful not to exhaust the prospect's patience.

The direct appeal. This is a risky method for closing which should be used only as a last resort. In effect, rather than waiting for the customer to make up his mind, the salesman does it for him. He asks directly for the order and might say something like this: "I have explained everything you wanted to know about the product. It is exactly what you need, and you know that it will save you money. You have followed my recommendations in the past and have never been disappointed. I assure you that you can do it again for I know you will be satisfied. If you have any additional questions or doubts, I'll be happy to clear them up. If not, then let's go ahead and I can have the installers here tomorrow." Successful use of this method is dependent upon excellent rapport with the prospect, knowing precisely what he needs and wants, and a record of satisfied service to build on. Also, the salesman must be sincere and know that what he promises is certain to materialize.

True or false?

_____ 1. When a product is selling very rapidly, it is often effective to point out that supply is limited and the prospect should act now.

_____ 2. If a customer wants an item, but in slightly different form, an effective close is to offer to change the item to meet his expectations.

_____ 3. Hesitant prospects can often be sold by letting them use an item on a trial basis.

_____ 4. The direct appeal should be used in most cases.

Now turn to Answer Frame 4[11] on page 60 to check your answers.

Frame 5[11]

Special techniques for closing

The salesman has a wide choice of methods to close the sale, and he will generally use them in combination rather than adhering to one single method. There are also a variety of techniques which will help to be more effective in closing. Some of the common ones are as follows:

Prevention of objection. An experienced salesman will anticipate common objections that will be raised at the time of closing, and he will attempt to say or do something to prevent them from occurring. For example, if he determines that the prospect is a procrastinator, he might prevent this problem from occurring by saying,

"Your problem is a serious one, and I know that you want to solve it as quickly as possible." The prospect generally will not disagree with such a statement, and at the same time the salesman has taken steps to minimize subsequent procrastination. Another example could be, "I know on the basis of how you operate that quality is more important to you than price." Such a statement is designed to prevent or minimize the prospect's objecting to price later in the sale.

Narrowing the choice. Another effective technique is to narrow the choice. Sometimes the prospect wants the product, but he does not buy it because he cannot decide which style or model he wants. He often is in a state of complete con-

Answer frame 4¹¹

1. True. This technique is known as the "limited supply" method for closing and should only be used when it is true that the item is in short supply.
2. True. Slight alterations often spell the difference between success and failure in closing a sale. However, the salesman should always be certain the changes can be made and at a profit for the firm.
3. True. A trial offer is particularly effective when there is no obligation on the part of the buyer, for it gives him a chance to determine for himself if the product will fulfill his needs.
4. False. The direct appeal is a risky method and should only be used as a last resort.

If you missed any of the above, you should restudy Frame 4¹¹ before turning to Frame 5¹¹ on page 59.

Frame 5¹¹ continued

fusion because he can't see the forest for the trees. For example, in selling a pair of shoes the salesman will usually confuse the prospect if he shows him from 15 to 20 pairs of shoes. A more appropriate approach is to carefully determine the prospect's needs and preferences and to narrow his choice to two or three pairs.

Emphasizing key features. Some prospects may be interested in a product because it has a unique or different feature—the first car with an automatic transmission, the first self-cleaning oven, an original figurine, the only lot on the street with a particular view, and so on. A special feature is of great importance to many prospects and may be the single factor which causes him to buy. If a prospect is so motivated, the salesman should agree, compliment him on his choice, and emphasize how the product is uniquely different from all others.

Handling a third party. It is sometimes difficult to close a sale when another person appears on the scene. It may be a small child who interrupts by asking questions or detracting the parent's attention by crying or becoming unruly. The salesman should be prepared for such incidents, which can occur in the prospect's home or in a business establishment. He might handle them by saying, "I have children of my own and know how tired they can get. If your mother doesn't object, I have a stick of sugarless gum that you might enjoy. And if you'll be good for a few more minutes, I just might give you another one." In other cases, the interrupting party may be an adult who asks questions which have already been covered; or worse, he criticizes the product. Such occur-

rences should not surprise or frustrate the salesman. He should plan in advance how to handle them and be prepared for the unexpected.

Getting the signature or approval. When the time arrives for the prospect to sign for the product or service, he often becomes tense and nervous. The salesman can help prepare him for this moment in the following ways:

The salesman can get the prospect to relax by having him sit down, or by offering him a cigarette, a cup of coffee, or a carbonated drink.

The contract or order form should be brought out before the close. It can be referred to when discussing guarantees and warranties and should be a part of the presentation.

The salesman can get a pen in the prospect's hand prior to the close by having him calculate what his savings will be.

The salesman should handle the contract in a natural and relaxed manner.

The prospect should be reassured that he is making a wise choice. If possible, the salesman should offer to take the product back without charge if the prospect is not satisfied.

What to do if the prospect doesn't buy. It is a fact of life that the salesman will usually make more presentations than sales. Depending upon the product or service being sold and the skill and experience of the salesman, he may have to make two, three, or even more calls to get one sale. However, when closes fail, the salesman must not become angry or argumentative with the prospect. Instead, he tries to retain and build good will. He thanks the prospect for the interview. He mentions that he will be in the area again at some future date and will be happy to call again. He leaves his card and other materials and encourages the prospect to call him if he can be of service. He might even give the prospect a small gift as a token of his appreciation for the time the prospect has spent with him. And he follows up by writing a brief note, mailing additional material, or telephoning. The salesman should also attempt to analyze why his close failed and determine ways and means to prevent this from happening again. And most important of all, he should always remember that failure is more common than success, but success can be achieved through confidence and persistent effort.

True or False?

_____ 1. An experienced salesman will anticipate common objections and will attempt to prevent or forestall them.

_____ 2. A salesman should always show a prospect his complete line of goods to assure that the prospect gets exactly what he wants.

_____ 3. If a salesman fails to make a sale, he should follow up by writing a brief note, sending additional material, or making a brief phone call.

_____ 4. A salesman should alter his methods significantly if after making a thorough presentation and overcoming all objections, a prospect does not buy.

Now turn to Answer Frame 5¹¹ on page 62 to check your answers.

Answer frame 5¹¹ ──────────────────────────────────────

1. True. By anticipating objections, a salesman may offer a counter argument *before* the objection, since this effectively blocks the prospect from raising such objections.
2. False. A more appropriate approach is to carefully determine the prospect's needs and preferences and to narrow his choice to two or three items.
3. True. A salesman should be friendly and helpful in all situations. A prospect who does not buy now may be quite receptive a month from now when his situation has changed.
4. False. In almost all areas of selling, the salesman is more likely to lose the sale than gain it. Each presentation should be a learning device so that a salesman can do better the next time. Some change in methods might be indicated, but not necessarily.

If you missed any of the above, you should restudy Frame 5¹¹ before beginning Chapter 12 below.

chapter 12

CUSTOMER RELATIONS

Frame 1¹² ──────────────────────────────────────

Today, selling takes place in a marketing-oriented economy in which the consumer is king. Successful selling is dependent upon repeat sales; and repeat sales in turn, depend upon having customers who are fully satisfied. The salesman, then, not only must sell customers the first time, but must do so in a manner that will create goodwill and a continuing relationship based on satisfaction of customer needs and wants.

How to develop good relations with customers

Serve rather than sell. The attitude that the salesman has about customers will greatly determine how well he will serve them. He must practice the golden rule and treat them as he himself

would want to be treated. In other words, he should sell as he would wish to be sold. In the long run, the salesman's best interests and those of the customer are the same. By serving the customer to the best of his ability, the salesman stands to gain.

Good customer relations begin by selling the customer a product or service which satisfies him. This means that the objective of the presentation is not solely making a sale in order to get a commission. More important to continued success is ability to fulfill the customer's needs and to help solve his problems. The salesman should fit the sale to the customer, even if it means selling less than the customer thinks he needs, or in some cases not selling to him at all. Such selling is based on complete honesty and a sincere desire to serve the buyer. If a customer knows that the salesman operates in this manner, he will trust him and follow his recommendations. From this standpoint, then, good customer relations are developed by serving rather than selling.

Postsale instructions and helpful suggestions. Even if the customer is sold the appropriate product or service, he sometimes becomes dissatisfied because he used it in an incorrect manner. Therefore, after the sale has been made, the salesman should make certain that the customer knows how to use and operate the product properly. He explains, demonstrates, and then has the customer go through the process to make certain he knows what he is doing. He also tells the customer to call him immediately if there is something he has forgotten or doesn't understand. And even if the customer doesn't contact him, the salesman still should make a call to determine how everything is going. Such a follow-up minimizes problems that might occur and also demonstrates that the salesman is genuinely concerned.

In addition, the salesman should give the customer helpful suggestions that will increase his satisfaction in using the product. For example, after selling a battery, the salesman might men-

tion that the life of the battery will be prolonged by regularly checking its water level. Or after selling a knit suit, he can mention that care should be taken to avoid snagging on rough surfaces. Or in selling paint, he should give the customer a free mixing stick and also explain how to mix or thin the paint. Customers appreciate receiving such helpful hints, and they can greatly increase his satisfaction with the product or service.

Reassure the customer. The product the customer has purchased may be perfectly appropriate for him, but later he may begin to doubt the wisdom of his purchase. Such feelings can develop when payments commence on the product, or when someone else compares his product with the one the prospect has purchased. This is often a natural reaction—particularly after the newness of the product has worn off—and the salesman should take steps to prevent it from occurring. Consequently, at the end of the sale, he should reassure the customer that he has made a wise choice. He should also refer to later comparisons that might be made to competitive products and explain how the product he has purchased is superior to the others.

Indicate whether each of the following statements is true or false by writing "T" or "F" in the space provided.

_____ 1. A salesman should always keep in mind that his primary objective is to "make the sale."
_____ 2. The salesman's job is ended when the sale is made.
_____ 3. A salesman can greatly enhance the value of a product to a buyer by explaining alternate uses, instructions for care, and so on.
_____ 4. Customers often have "second thoughts" about products and services and need to be reassured as to the wisdom of their choice.

Now turn to Answer Frame 1¹² on page 64 to check your responses.

Frame 2¹²

Look for unrelated ways to help the customer. The salesman will naturally want to give the customer helpful information related to the product or service purchased. However, he should also try to serve the customer in other ways if he possibly can. For example, if a customer mentions going on a trip and doesn't know the best route to take,

the salesman who recently made the same trip might be able to give him some helpful suggestions. Or if the customer comments about his failure to grow roses and the salesman knows the cause of his problems, he should devote some time to telling him what to do. In offering such information the salesman should:

Answer frame 1¹²

1. False. The salesman's primary objective should be to fulfill his customer's needs and to help solve his problems. He must accomplish this even if it means selling less than the customer thinks he needs or, in some cases, not selling him at all.

2. False. At the end of a sale, a salesman should make certain that the customer knows how to properly use and operate the product. This process may last long after the sale is made.

3. True. Customers appreciate receiving helpful hints about the use and care of products and they can greatly increase his satisfaction with them.

4. True. Feelings of doubt often develop when payments start or when someone else compares his product with the one the customer has purchased. A salesman must follow up his sales with reassurances that the customer has made a good decision.

If you missed any of the above, you should restudy Frame 1¹² before turning to Frame 2¹² on page 63.

Frame 2¹² continued

Be humble in his approach and avoid conveying the impression that he is an expert.

Be careful not to embarrass the customer.

Be certain that he knows what he is talking about.

Avoid advising the customer to do something if there is a possibility that the outcome might be different than he promises.

Refrain from offering unrelated advice or service as a means to obligate the customer.

And he should not become so involved in referring to and doing other things that such activity interferes with his effectiveness as a salesman. His main job is to sell his product, and he should not let the tail wag the dog.

Express appreciation. Customers not only want to be served well, but they also want to be appreciated. Therefore, the salesman should always thank the customer for his patronage. Expressions of appreciation need not be long and drawn out. Such statements as the following might be used:

"It has been a pleasure visiting with you, Mr. Doe, and please call me if you have any further questions."

"I appreciate your order, Mr. Doe, and am looking forward to working with you."

"I thank you for the time you have given me, Mr. Doe, and greatly appreciate your patronage."

Such statements should be warm and sincere, and it is appropriate for the salesman to shake the customer's hand as he expresses them. A short follow-up letter is also an excellent gesture for expressing appreciation.

Remember and recognize customers. Little acts of kindness are important in developing good customer relations. There are many instances where the salesman can demonstrate that he genuinely cares for and takes an active interest in his customers. He can express these feelings in some of the following ways:

Send the customer a card on his birthday, an anniversary date, and so on.

Send the customer a card and/or gift if he or members of his family are ill or hospitalized.

Write the customer a note of congratulations if he has been promoted, has received a special award, if his name has appeared in the news, and so on.

Send the customer a Christmas card and/or a small gift as a token of appreciation for his patronage.

Customers appreciate being remembered and recognized and the salesman should always be thoughtful about their problems and successes.

Develop a professional reputation. Customers must like and respect the salesman if he is to gain their trust and confidence. Some of the ways he can build such a relationship is by keeping private information confidential. The customer should not be reluctant to talk honestly with the salesman; and he in turn, should not betray this confidence. He should also refrain from attacking or criticizing others. Speak well of someone or don't talk about him at all should generally be his motto. The salesman who talks maliciously about others often conveys the impression that he talks about everyone (including the customer himself) in the same manner. In addition, it is most important for the salesman to be truthful and honest. If delivery cannot be made when promised, then the salesman should explain this to the buyer regardless of how disappointed he might be. There is no substitute for complete honesty, and the salesman should always practice it. Finally, he should always be reliable, considerate, and courteous. A customer generally will not forsake a salesman who treats him fairly and honestly.

Handle complaints properly. The first principle for handling complaints is to listen to what the customer has to say. Don't interrupt or contradict; instead thank him for bringing the problem to your attention and let him get it completely "off his chest." Second, ask or analyze what can be done to remedy the situation. Then, determine if the proposed solution or settlement is agreeable with the customer. And finally, follow through and make certain that what you promised is done. There is nothing more annoying than to find something wrong with the product and then not being able to have it corrected. Most customer complaints are justifiable, and ill feelings generally will be avoided if the salesman is prompt and courteous in handling such matters.

Entertaining. The amount and kind of entertaining a salesman does will vary with the type of selling in which he is engaged and the amount of money that is available for such purposes. In many types of selling, entertaining is not the custom; but in some situations it is expected, and customers may feel slighted if they are not entertained. The importance of the account and the time and money the salesman has for entertaining should be the main factors for determining which customers and prospects should be entertained. Such entertaining should also be done in a spirit of sincere appreciation and friendliness rather than as a means to obligate the customer.

Holding accounts. Successful selling is continued selling to a satisfied customer. It begins by selling him the right product, at the right price, at the right time, and in the right amounts. And it continues by calling on him regularly and by fulfilling his needs. The salesman must not rest on his laurels and erroneously conclude that once the sale has been made, the buyer will automatically remain loyal and faithful to him. On the contrary, competition is extremely fierce, and customers will buy another product if they become dissatisfied with a certain product or service. Consequently, the salesman must be constantly alert for any signals that might indicate that his customer is becoming dissatisfied or is beginning to drift away from him. Common signals to watch for are:

A gradual or sudden drop in sales.

Increased complaints about the product or service.

More frequent reference to competitors' products and their respective advantages.

Illness or inability of the customer to manage his business properly.

Changes in the customer's business policies or personnel.

His being out of his office more than he should be when the salesman calls, with the salesman finding it increasingly more difficult to see him.

Outside factors such as legislation, economic conditions, obsolescence, and so on, which can affect his continuance as a customer.

The salesman should carefully watch for such changes and do everything he possibly can to correct or adjust to them. And in those cases where he loses the account, he should determine why, how, when, and to whom the account was lost. The answers might help to prevent the problem from occurring with other customers and also give the salesmen some ideas for regaining the lost account.

Label each of the following statements as true or false.

_____ 1. A salesman should end a presentation or sale by expressing appreciation for having had the opportunity to discuss his products or services.

_____ 2. It is usually a good practice to criticize other salesmen and products so that the customer does not look around for alternative choices.

_____ 3. Customer complaints should be listened to and handled promptly with little debate from the salesman.

_____ 4. Once a salesman has obtained a customer, he can be fairly certain that the customer will stay with him.

Now turn to Answer Frame 2¹² on page 68 to check your responses.

chapter 13

ETHICS IN SELLING

Frame 1¹³

Ethics has to do with the moral principles governing conduct—with what constitutes "good" actions and practices. What is "good" is generally evaluated according to some standard or code of ethics, either self-imposed or created by a society or some group within it, such as a profession or organization. Salesmen, too, have their personal and professional standards of conduct, and we will discuss some aspects of ethics in selling in this chapter.

A major question debated by all concerned with ethical problems over the years has been that of absolute versus relative moral standards. Some believe that such things as absolutes—rules that apply always and under all circumstances—exist in moral conduct; others hold that only relative ethics are possible—that is, that what is good

necessarily varies with the time, the circumstances, and the situation.

Like most people living in a changing and imperfect world, the salesman does not try to establish moral absolutes but rather strives to be as honest and professional as he can in the situation in which he finds himself. He recognizes that there are too many different types and levels of selling, too many complex sales situations, to always be able to say categorically that what is ethical and good in one will be applicable to all. Each sales situation must be studied to evaluate what will contribute to the good of all concerned, not just in the short run but over a period of time. When situations are relatively simple and straightforward, it is easier to find the ethical solution. But in our highly competitive market economy, services and products to be sold have become increasingly complicated and technical. Because of the growing complexity of the environment in which selling takes place, the salesman finds it ever more difficult, as well as more relevant and important, to practice ethical conduct.

To say that salesmen operate under a code of relative rather than absolute ethics is not to imply that ethics should be any less important in selling. On the contrary, because consumerism is a rising important force in the marketplace today, profit making can no longer be pursued by business to the exclusion of ethical and social consideration. Business must also be concerned with its social responsibilities to the consumer, to its workers, to the community, and to the nation as a whole. It is true that American business still operates in a competitive economy. However, the code of the social Darwinism, emphasizing survival of the fittest, is no longer acceptable. Competition today must be tempered with a social conscience. Higher levels of education and improved methods of communication have contributed to making man more aware of his social responsibilities. In addition, over half of our total population today is composed of people who are under 35 years of age. This predominantly younger group of consumers holds different ideas and tends to question past and existing practices. Ethics are, therefore, of increasing importance to the salesman, and he should be fully informed as to how they relate to his particular activities.

The salesman's responsibility to the consumer

The ethical salesman will make it the major objective of his selling to *serve and satisfy* the consumer. In everyday practice this means that the salesman should never sell the customer something he does not need. The product or service should be specifically geared to, and appropriate for, the customer; and if it will not benefit him, it is the salesman's responsibility to so inform him. In other words, fulfilling the customer's needs or solving his problems is regarded as being of greater importance to the salesman than the commission he can earn in making the sale.

To provide dedicated service to the consumer,

the salesman must keep informed on his product or service. Inadequate product knowledge can result in both ineffective and detrimental selling. In the case of a doctor, if he does not fully understand the effects of a drug, he can carelessly make a decision which could cause the death of his patient. In like fashion, the salesman can harm the customer by giving him erroneous or inadequate information about the product and by failing to understand or by not caring about the customer's problems. Therefore, a salesman who practices good ethics will refrain from making misleading, false, or uninformed statements about his product or service. He will also avoid using flattery, bribes, or high-pressure tactics to influence customers. Nor will he betray customer confidences or engage in personal gossip about his customers or others.

The salesman's responsibility to his company

An ethical salesman will also recognize his moral responsibilities to his company. Many salesmen have expense accounts and are easily tempted to "pad expenses." This practice, along with using company cars, equipment, and supplies for personal use, not only is dishonest but also greatly increases the costs of doing business. This ultimately can harm the salesman himself as well as the company. The company also pays and relies on an individual to perform a given job. Consequently, if the salesman works at less than his capacity, he is shortchanging his employer and simultaneously hurting himself in terms of personal growth and advancement.

Other unethical practices which are injurious to the company are faking customer reports, withholding vital information which the company needs, failure to use new tools or information provided by the company, and deliberately delaying sales until the company sponsors a contest. Sometimes an unscrupulous salesman, in violation of company policy, will resort to lavish entertainment or the use of bribes to get business. Such practices have very damaging effects when less favored customers learn about them; and although the salesman is the one at fault, his actions also create an unfavorable image for the company.

Answer frame 2¹²

1. True. Statements of appreciation should be warm and sincere regardless of the outcome of the presentation. A short follow-up letter is also an excellent way of expressing appreciation.
2. False. A salesman should always speak well of other people and products and be truthful and honest in his dealings. This will result in a feeling of trust and confidence from prospects and customers.
3. True. A salesman should listen to complaints, determine what is equitable to both parties, propose a remedy and see if it is acceptable, and follow through to assure that action has been taken.
4. False. Competition is fierce for most products and services, and a customer will buy from someone else if he becomes dissatisfied with his present product or the service he is receiving.

If you missed any of the above, you should reread Frame 2¹² before beginning Chapter 13 on page 66.

Frame 1¹³ continued

Some salesmen will occasionally have a second job on the side. There is nothing wrong with having extra outside employment as long as it does not interfere with one's major job. However, it usually is very difficult to avoid "burning the candle at both ends," and the attention required by a second job will generally interfere with the salesman's effectiveness in his principal one. Another related problem is for the salesman to be involved in outside activities which represent a conflict of interest. Examples of this would be a salesman who sells newspaper advertising and also serves on the board of directors of the local radio station, or a salesman who sells plastic products and also has a financial interest in a wood product company. Generally, no man can serve two masters at the same time, and he is usually required to make a choice between the two.

Some companies make a practice of pirating salesmen from other companies, particularly if the salesman is employed by a company which is a leader in its field and has an excellent training program. The salesman is free to seek different employment. However, when he is working for one employer, he should give that employer a full day's work and not betray his confidence. He should also give the company advance notice if he plans to accept another job, in order that his employer may have adequate time to find a replacement. In addition, all equipment and supplies belonging to the company should be returned, as should customer files, since they technically belong to the company and are needed by the person who will replace him.

Indicate whether each of the following statements is true or false by writing "T" or "F" in the space provided.

_____ 1. Salesmen usually operate under a system of *absolute* ethics that are always applicable in any situation.

_____ 2. Salesmen must always remember that the sole purpose of operating a business is to make a profit for the owners.

_____ 3. A salesman must occasionally make misleading, false, or uninformed statements about his products in order to make a sale.

_____ 4. A salesman has ethical responsibilities to his prospects and customers but not to his company.

Now turn to Answer Frame 1¹³ on page 70 to check your responses.

Frame 2[13]

The salesman's responsibility to his competitors

It may appear strange that the salesman has a responsibility to his competitors; one would think that the salesman's only responsibility to those competing with him would be to outsell them. It is true that he will attempt to outsell his competitors; however, he must do it in an ethical and professional manner. In actual practice this means that the salesman will emphasize the positive points of his own product or service rather than constantly "knocking" the competition. He will refrain from making misleading or false statements about the competitor's product, and also will not circulate any false rumors about its operations or salesmen. Such practices may give the salesman a temporary advantage, but ultimately the truth will be known, and then the salesman will usually lose the confidence of the customer and of others as well. In some instances some salesmen have been known to sabotage or damage competitor products in an attempt to increase their own sales. Needless to say, such actions are not only unethical but illegal as well, and any person who resorts to such desperate measures has no business selling. Resorting to such actions is usually caused by the salesman's own insecurity and lack of ability, and such persons usually remain in selling for a very short period.

The salesman's responsibility to his fellow salesmen

The salesman also has a responsibility to his fellow salesmen. He should share information with them and be willing to help them out on certain problems. In the case of new or beginning salesmen, he should volunteer his services to help them learn their jobs. The salesman is an individualist, but he must also work cooperatively with the other salesmen. They must work together as members of a team. For if they work together and help each other the company will prosper and grow. And if the company prospers and grows, the individual salesman will prosper with it.

Other ethical practices are to refrain from stealing sales from other salesmen and to avoid criticizing them in the presence of customers. The medical and legal professions are very strict in adhering to this standard, and salesmen should also practice it.

The salesman's responsibility to the government and society

As previously mentioned, business can no longer be regarded as an island unto itself with profit making as its sole objective. On the contrary, business activities today are recognized as being closely related with how we will live and the type of society we will live in. Our government has stepped in to protect the interests of society, and there are many laws affecting business practices. These laws, discussed in Chapter 6, relate not only to manufacturing of the product but such other aspects as pricing, discounts, allowances, advertising, warranties, and guarantees. The salesman has a duty to be informed about these laws and to honor them. In addition, he should be concerned about the use of his product or service as it relates to society as a whole. He is not just an employee of a company, but a member of the human race who should be as concerned as anyone else about such social problems as unemployment, pollution, crime, war, and poverty.

The salesman owes something to himself and his family

Finally, the salesman has a responsibility to himself and to his family. He should select selling work which is of real interest to him and commensurate with his abilities. Otherwise he may take out his frustrations and emotional upsets on his family and jeopardize his own health and happiness. If he likes his job and is good at it, he will not only help himself and his family but will make a greater contribution to society as a whole.

The salesman has an obligation to keep himself in good physical and mental condition. Furthermore, he should keep himself challenged and motivated in order to avoid leveling off in a state of indifference and complacency as sometimes

Answer frame 1¹³

1. False. Salesmen usually operate under a system of *relative* ethics, for it is virtually impossible to develop a single code of ethics that would cover all selling situations.
2. False. Profit is no longer the sole purpose of operating a business. Businesses must also be concerned with their social obligations to the consumer, to their workers, to the community, and to the nation as a whole.
3. False. An ethical salesman will refrain from making misleading, false, or uninformed statements, nor will he betray customer confidences.
4. False. A salesman should be ethical about his expense account, his car and equipment, his sales reports, and all other relationships with his company.

If you missed any of the above, you should restudy Frame 1¹³ before turning to Frame 2¹³ on page 69.

Frame 2¹³ continued

happens to seasoned salesmen who become content and cease striving to improve themselves.

Insofar as his family is concerned, he should remember that his effectiveness in selling greatly determines their social and economic status. What he does in selling will affect the care they will receive, where and the type of home they will live in, the comforts they will enjoy, and the degree of education they will receive. He is a provider in every respect, and his family relies and depends upon him.

In summary, ethics are the morals or principles we practice in doing our work. The basic philosophy underlying an acceptable code of ethics can best be expressed in these words: "Do unto others, as you would have others do unto you." Being ethical requires that the salesman maintain a consideration of others, including his company, his fellow salesmen, competitors, society, and his family. In this way he will not only be an ethical salesman, but a more successful one who has also helped to make a meaningful contribution to the world in which he lives.

Label each of the following statements as true or false.

_____ 1. A salesman usually can gain a competitive edge over other salesmen by "knocking" the other man's goods and services.

_____ 2. In his efforts for promotion, a salesman should avoid helping other salesmen because they might get the promotion instead.

_____ 3. The salesman has a commitment to society and cannot separate himself from society's needs.

_____ 4. The salesman's responsibility to his family is incompatible with his responsibility to his work.

Now turn to Answer Frame 2¹³ on page 72 to check your answers.

chapter 14

PERSONAL PLANNING AND CONTROL

Frame 1¹⁴

More than most occupations, selling permits a large measure of self-direction. Assuming that selling efforts must be planned and controlled—and certainly success in selling can be achieved in no other way—the salesman cannot rely on others always to direct his work for him. Planning and control for the salesman is largely a "do-it-yourself" activity. The self-directed salesman is himself mainly responsible for determining what success he will achieve. His internal motivations—his ambition and drive—must be strong enough to keep him on the job and giving his best without external prodding. He must be capable of setting his own goals. He thinks clearly, plans, analyzes, and organizes his work. He has the necessary determination, persistence, and self-discipline to forge ahead regardless of obstacles. He is capable of adapting to changing circumstances, and he works constantly for self-improvement.

Establishing work goals

The salesman will find it helpful to begin by forming a long-range plan as to what he wants to be and accomplish in life. He should have some idea what salary he plans to make next year, within 5 years, 10 years, and so on, until the time he retires. He should also have some idea of the position he hopes to have when he finally retires. Other considerations affecting the salesman's goals and plans are the type of home he wishes to live in, how many children he will have, where he will send them to college, what he plans to do on

vacations, where and when he plans to travel, and the possessions he eventually hopes to own.

It is true that one cannot expect life to go precisely as planned, for there are many uncontrollable variables, such as unavoidable illness, general economic conditions, unexpected misfortunes, and other unforeseen events which will greatly alter one's original plans. Yet, a self-directed man cannot completely resign himself to fate and blithely say, "Come what may." Such a person lets time, circumstances, and others manage him, rather than managing himself. To plan and manage your life means to have some goals and dreams of your own. It means that although you realize other factors can greatly change and modify your life, you still have some personal goals and purposes which motivate you to achieve and succeed. A salesman's goals therefore determine his degree of motivation; and accordingly, his motivation greatly determines what he is and will become.

In addition to being "goal-oriented," the self-directed person will plan and organize for fulfilling his goals. In selling, this amounts to establishing personal sales quotas for the year, season, month, and in some cases, the week or day. Then these sales quotas must be related to types of products and the number of customers to whom he plans to sell.

Many salesmen evaluate their performance by computing a "performance index" figure which is arrived at by dividing actual sales by planned or expected sales. For example, if the salesman

Answer frame 2¹³

1. False. "Knocking" the competition might give a salesman a temporary advantage, but ultimately such a salesman will lose the confidence of prospects and customers.
2. False. A salesman is the member of a team, and by working together the team and the company will prosper and grow. A salesman working alone cannot possibly accomplish what a cohesive corporate effort can do.
3. True. As a member of society, a salesmen must be concerned with matters such as unemployment, pollution, crime, war, and poverty.
4. False. These two responsibilities are compatible. A salesman should be happy with his work and work productively to assure his family a healthy and wholesome environment. Of course, it is possible to ignore the family or the work by devoting too much time to the other.

If you missed any of the above, you should reread Frame 2¹³ before beginning Chapter 14 on page 71.

Frame 1¹⁴ continued

planned or expected his sales to be $10,000, $15,000, and $20,000 for the months of January, February, and March respectively, and his actual sales were $10,000, $13,500, and $22,500 for these three months; his performance index (P.I.) would be 100% for January, 90% for February, and 112½% for March. This calculation helps the salesman to see how closely he achieved his monthly goals and also gives him some definite figures for determining what changes he will have to make if he intends to fulfill his expected volume for the entire year. It is much better to determine where you stand each week or month, when there is still time to make changes, rather than waiting until the end of the year, when it is too late to do anything about it. In other words, the "self-managed" salesman will plan frequently and periodically rather than just once or twice a year.

In addition to annual and monthly sales volumes, the salesman should analyze such other *quantitative* aspects as:

a) Sales volume breakdowns based on product lines; geographic areas or territories; types of customers; whether the sale is made by mail, telephone, or in person; cash or charge sales; and so on.
b) The number and average size of orders.
c) The average number of calls made to secure and service an order.
d) Amount of sales increase derived from selling more to existing accounts or from securing new accounts, and amount of sales decrease resulting from lost accounts.

Much of this information is provided by management and given to the salesman on a periodic basis. It is important not to view the collection and analysis of such data as so-called "busy work." For the salesman must first pinpoint his weaknesses and analyze their causes if he is to do an effective job of improving his performance.

If the salesman plans to increase his business each year, he must *sell more to existing accounts* and also *secure new accounts*. Generally, there is greater opportunity for increasing sales by securing new accounts, for if the salesman is doing an effective job with existing accounts, they ordinarily will be buying the maximum amount they can purchase from him. Consequently, he must devote a certain amount of time each week or month to securing new accounts. At the same time, he must continue to serve his existing customers adequately for if he fails to give them the attention they warrant, he may end up losing more accounts than he gains. It must also be remembered that the salesman will automatically lose some customers each year. People move, retire, die, change jobs, or other situations occur which cause them to cancel accounts. It can be readily seen from these circumstances that the more successful a salesman becomes, the busier he becomes. And this is as it should be, for there is no easy shortcut to success; it is generally measured in terms of effort and work.

Indicate whether each of the following statements is true or false by writing "T" or "F" in the space provided.

_____ 1. The self-managed salesman must plan his work and work his plan.

_____ 2. A self-managed salesman's goals should be solely based on the company's goals because the company is his source of compensation.

_____ 3. Sales quotas for salesmen should be established yearly because the company's quotas are usually yearly projections.

_____ 4. A salesman may evaluate his performance by computing a "performance index" calculated by dividing actual sales by planned sales.

_____ 5. A salesman achieves the greatest success by securing new accounts only.

Now turn to Answer Frame 1[14] on page 74 to check your responses.

Frame 2[14]

Controlling selling time and energy

Considerable time is spent in preparing for a sale, traveling, and waiting to see prospects. The salesman spends only about 20 percent of his time in face-to-face selling, and the remainder is devoted to other related activities. Consequently, time is money, and the salesman must carefully plan and control it.

To make better use of his time the salesman should analyze each of his customers in terms of their annual sales, miles traveled to reach them, number of visits per year, and other expenses connected with each account. In many sales organizations it is not uncommon to find that as few as 20 or 25 percent of the customers account for as much as 75 percent or 80 percent of the total sales volume. This does not mean that smaller accounts should be eliminated or ignored. On the contrary, the successful salesman should and will have all sizes and types of accounts. However, he should allocate his time in proportion to the size and potential of the account.

Other means the salesman can use to make better use of his time are to shorten his presentation and avoid needless repetition. Some salesmen say the same thing over and over again until they sound like a broken record. This is not selling, but a diffusion of meaningless words. Instead, the salesman should carefully analyze the prospect's needs and concentrate on those points in making his presentation. It should always be remembered that an effective presentation is not judged by how many words are spoken, but rather by what is said and also how well it is said.

Idle talking or gossiping is another thief of time. It is very easy for the salesman to become involved in conversations about something he is personally interested in—particularly with congenial and likable customers. Such discussions can be about the salesman's hobbies, his family, sports, the war, politics, or other situations which are of real interest to him. From time to time a certain amount of his conversations with customers will naturally be about these topics, for he should be well informed and interested in many things. However, he should guard against talking too much about such matters at the expense of his productivity in selling. He should always remember that he is a professional salesman and his main job is to serve and sell.

Valuable time is also wasted by getting started late in the morning, taking unduly long coffee breaks, taking a long lunch, and quitting early. For example, on the basis of a 40-hour week, let us suppose that a salesman starts at 8:45 A.M. rather than 8:00 A.M.; that he takes two coffee breaks lasting a half hour each rather than 15 minutes; that he takes an hour and a half for lunch rather than one hour; that he spends approximately 45 minutes each day in idle or needless conversation; that he spends approximately 45 minutes each day attending to personal business such as picking up groceries, shopping, and so on; and that he quits at 4:15 P.M. rather than 5:00 P.M. Such a schedule results in approximately four lost hours each

Answer frame 1¹⁴

1. True. A self-managed salesman has goals and the desire to succeed, he knows how to plan and organize, he has determination, and he knows how to adapt to different situations.
2. False. A salesman must establish goals for his life that take into consideration his family, his personal satisfactions, and society as well as his employer.
3. False. A salesman must establish quotas for each season, month, week, and day in order to maintain a "goal-oriented" life style. Yearly quotas are too broad to provide the incentive needed for day-to-day motivation.
4. True. The "performance index" is calculated by dividing actual sales by planned or expected sales. A salesman should aim for a P.I. of 100 percent or better each month.
5. False. If a salesman plans to increase his sales, he must sell more to existing accounts as well as securing new accounts.

If you missed any of the above, you should restudy Frame 1¹⁴ before turning to Frame 2¹⁴ on page 73.

Frame 2¹⁴ continued

day, representing half of the salesman's total (working) time. This is altogether **too** much lost time, and any salesman who has habits like this should learn how to schedule himself more efficiently.

True or false?

_____ 1. Salesmen spend most of their time in face-to-face selling.

_____ 2. Salesmen should concentrate their efforts on the major customers and not waste their time calling on small accounts.

_____ 3. Salesmen often get involved in idle conversations which waste their time as well as the customer's.

_____ 4. It is easy to lose half a day in seemingly harmless diversions that rob a salesman of his productivity.

Now turn to Answer Frame 2¹⁴ on page 76 to check your answers.

Frame 3¹⁴

Much time is also lost in finding excuses for not going out to sell on a particular day. Typical alibis for each of the months sometimes are as follows:

January—Too soon after Christmas and people have no money.

February—Too cold.

March—Unpredictable weather. The roads are often muddy making it difficult to travel.

April—Customers too busy with spring planting, cleaning, and repairing the ravages of winter.

May—Too many customers afflicted with spring fever.

June—Time for swimming, boating, fishing, and gala summer weddings.

July—Too hot.

August—Vacation time.

September—Back to school time. Customers also too busy preparing for winter.

October—Football games, hunting, and time to enjoy the fall season.

November—Lots of sickness and colds because of colder weather.

December—Customers too busy preparing for Christmas.

The salesman who falls back on the excuse that people are busy will accomplish nothing, for they are always busy except when they are ill, asleep, or deceased. The productive salesman, however, will have definite goals and will attempt to fulfill them regardless of the circumstances that might prevail.

The salesman should also carefully check the amount of time he generally spends with each of his customers. In many cases, such an analysis will reveal that he has a tendency to concentrate on congenial customers and to avoid the difficult ones. It is only natural for a salesman to gravitate toward more likable customers; however, in terms of effective utilization of time it is more important for him to consider the amount the customer buys or his future potential.

Another common weakness is to continue calling on accounts that will never buy. The saying that "If at first you don't succeed, then try again," should certainly be practiced, for in most instances it requires several calls before a sale can be made. However, each call should be carefully planned to bring the salesman closer to the sale, and he should have a criteria for determining at what point he will discontinue his efforts. Moreover, such action should not be viewed as that of a "quitter." On the contrary, the salesman's time is a valuable commodity, and he should not waste it on prospects who will never buy.

Much time is spent in traveling and waiting to see customers. Rather than listening to the car radio or reading a magazine in the waiting room, the salesman can often use these times to learn more about his job. As he is driving, he can listen to tapes on selling which are played on small and inexpensive recording machines. Or he can carry reading material with him which pertains to various aspects of selling and read it while he is waiting to see prospects. He can also do some of his report writing or record keeping while waiting. The reader should not conclude from this discussion that the salesman should incessantly drive himself or keep himself busy every single minute of the day. Instead, he should work in a natural and relaxed manner, but at the same time be careful not to waste his time.

Daily plans

To avoid wasted calls and actions, the salesman should carefully plan each day's work in advance. Following are the items he should consider:

a) Determine the persons who will be visited.
b) Consider where they are located and arranged the visits in a systematic order.
c) Review what had happened on previous visits.
d) Pinpoint the specific needs and problems of each customer or prospect.
e) Carefully determine what you plan to do, and the amount of time you will spend on each visit.
f) Gather and prepare materials specifically designed for each customer or prospect.

Careful planning in the beginning will minimize wasted time in the field. Selling is very comparable to flying a plane. Before the pilot takes off he must know where he is going, what bearing he will follow to reach his destination, how long it will take, at what speed he will travel, and prevailing weather conditions. He does not fly in a given direction and hope that he will eventually reach his destination. On the contrary, the whole flight is carefully planned and scheduled from its beginning to the very end. So it is with selling. Similarly, the salesman must carefully plan his day's activities in advance if he is to utilize his time effectively. Lost sales can easily happen, but successful ones must be carefully organized and planned.

Controlling expenses

So far sales have been the main measure mentioned for increasing productivity. However, at the same time, expenses must also be analyzed and controlled, for they are directly related to earnings and profits. General considerations for reducing expenses are to:

1. Analyze the size of each account in relation to the expenses to service it. These expenses should include the number of calls made per year, distance traveled, telephone and mailing costs, and special services provided. Such an analysis will often reveal that a disproportionate amount of time and money is often spent on less productive accounts.
2. Reduce traveling expenses by planning in advance, routing in a systematic manner, making

Answer frame 2¹⁴

1. False. Only about 20 percent of a salesman's time is spent in face-to-face selling; the remainder is spent on related activities such as travel, waiting, preparing reports, and so on.
2. False. The successful salesman calls on all sizes of accounts, but he allocates his time in proportion to the potential of each account.
3. True. It is very easy for a salesman to become involved in conversations about things he is interested in, and such discussions are often helpful in establishing rapport with customers. But a salesman must be very careful not to spend too much time on such matters.
4. True. A salesman who starts 15 minutes late, takes two half-hour coffee breaks, an extra half-hour lunch break, and spends 45 minutes to do some chores and talk with the customer's employees, and quits at 4:15 rather than 5:00 P.M. may lose half of his productive time each day and not be aware of it.

If you missed any of the above, you should restudy Frame 2¹⁴ before turning to Frame 3¹⁴ on page 74.

Frame 3¹⁴ continued

appointments, and using the telephone or mail to contact customers when possible.

3. Use advertising for increasing sales. It is usually an effecttve tool. However, the salesman should carefully plan and schedule his use of advertising, avoid needless duplication or repetition, and analyze its costs in relation to its objectives and/or sales generated.
4. Remember that written communications are less expensive and often more complete and accurate than telephone calls.

5. Eat well, but avoid luxury restaurants.
6. Stay in clean and comfortable hotels or motels and avoid the plush ones.
7. Be moderate in entertaining.

Management generally has explicit policies regarding these latter expenses. The salesman should also recognize that the expenses of operating a business are progressively higher each year, and he should work with management in a cooperative manner to help control them.

Label each of the following statements as true or false.

_____ 1. Many salesmen unknowingly waste their time calling on accounts which have little extra potential or none at all.

_____ 2. Much of a salesman's time is wasted in driving from customer to customer and waiting to see people, and there is nothing that he can do to make this time productive.

_____ 3. A salesman should not bother planning his day's activities because too many unforeseen factors may affect what he does.

_____ 4. A salesman has too many other more important duties than to bother with analyzing travel costs, expenses related to various accounts, and other such accounting problems.

Now turn to Answer Frame 3¹⁴ on page 78 to check your answers.

Frame 4¹⁴

Record keeping

Every business firm has to keep records in order to schedule orders and inventories, to plan production, and to determine its financial position. There would be complete chaos without them. A similar need for record keeping also applies to the salesman's activities, for records are an important tool for effective planning and utilization of his time.

Generally, two sets of records should be kept—one on *current customers* and another on *prospects*. The information to be recorded will vary with the type of product or service being sold. Items most frequently recorded are:

a) The customer's name, address, and telephone number.
b) The date of each visit.
c) The date, amount, and type of each sale.
d) The specific needs and problems of each customer or prospect.
e) Points emphasized by the salesman on each visit.
f) Other miscellaneous points.

The above listing is only a suggested one, and many other items can be added. However, the important point is for the salesman to keep some form of records. He makes hundreds of calls each year, and it is humanly impossible for him to remember everything that has happened. The increased use of computers helps to record much of the information needed by the salesman, but he still must maintain records of his own. There are a multitude of things to remember, and record keeping on a continuing basis is a necessary adjunct for efficient and successful selling. Salesmen also are frequently promoted from smaller to larger territories or to supervisory positions and should maintain records which will help the man who succeeds them.

Use of off-the-job time

What the salesman does outside his work is his own personal business. However, such activities will have a direct or indirect effect upon his work and he should evaluate them in terms of the extent to which they will help or hinder him in his performance as a salesman. In this respect, two general recommendations can be made. First, the salesman is not just a businessman. He is also a member of a community and should take an active part in its activities. This means belonging to certain groups and organizations, such as the Parent Teachers Association, a local church, the Chamber of Commerce, Kiwanis, the Rotary

Club, the local Citizen's Committee, a local farm bureau, and many others. It is his duty and responsibility as a parent and citizen to be active in such groups, for they help to improve our communities and nation. But it is not necessary for him to belong to everything. Actually, it is better to participate actively in a few organizations than to belong to many in name only. In some cases, a salesman can be involved in so many organizations that he is unable to devote adequate time to his work. Such a schedule should be avoided and he should limit himself to those organizations in which he can actively participate without interfering with his job. Such an arrangement not only allows him to make a contribution to his fellow man, but it can also help him to gain respect and stature in the community. The salesman should belong to professional organizations which are related to his particular type of selling. These organizations keep him informed as to what is happening in his particular area of selling, and also provide him with valuable information for improving his performance.

The second recommendation is to take time out for leisure activities. Like almost all types of work, selling has certain pressures. It is important for the salesman to periodically escape these tensions. He should set aside some time each week to pursue a hobby, to see a play, to watch a baseball or football game, to go hunting or fishing, to play golf, to go boating or swimming, or engage in other similar forms of recreation. Rather than detracting from his work, these activities serve to rejuvenate and make him more productive on the job. There is no shortcut to success; it is generally measured in terms of the effort an individual expends. However, it is equally important for him to take time out to relax, reflect, and rejuvenate himself.

Subjective evaluation

In order to improve his performance the salesman should also periodically evaluate himself on a subjective basis. This normally is done by using rating or self-evaluation forms which ask such questions as:

Do I know enough about my product or service?

Answer frame 3¹⁴

1. True. Salesmen have a tendency to call on congenial accounts and to avoid difficult ones. They also tend to spend too much time on accounts that are not moving closer to a sale. Therefore, a salesman must carefully evaluate each account to determine how much time he should spend with each.
2. False. Rather than listening to the car radio or reading a magazine in a waiting room, a salesman could put this time to work by keeping records, preparing reports, listening to educational cassette tapes, and/or analyzing his last presentation.
3. False. Careful daily plans will minimize wasted time in the field. Proper scheduling can minimize driving distances, and planning his objectives for each account will minimize unnecessary talk and delays.
4. False. Expenses are as important to profits as are sales. A salesman is responsible for determining, analyzing, and minimizing the costs associated with his job.

If you missed any of the above, you should reread Frame 3¹⁴ before turning to Frame 4¹⁴ on page 76.

Frame 4¹⁴ continued

Do I do an adequate job of preparing and organizing myself?

What type of image do I project in terms of my appearance and personality?

How effective is my approach?

How effective am I in "sizing up" the customer and in determining his needs and problems?

Do I generate self-confidence and enthusiasm?

How effective am I in dramatizing my product and in proving selling points?

How skillful am I in handling objections?

Do I know how to recognize closing signals?

How skillful am I in executing closes?

Do I follow up after each sale to make certain the customer is completely satisfied?

To what extent can I increase my productivity by better routing, shorter coffee breaks, and better record keeping?

Do I consistently try to secure a given number of new accounts each week or month, and how successful am I in achieving these goals?

Do I consistently try to improve my performance by reading articles on selling, taking courses, or attending sales meetings?

The above questions are typical of those that are commonly used in self-evaluation tests, and many more can be added. More complete evaluations can be obtained by having them made by other persons, such as the sales manager, the sales trainer, fellow salesmen, and customers. The important thing is that the salesman cannot improve himself unless he analyzes his weaknesses and experiments with methods to correct them. A salesman who wants to be a true professional will always try to evaluate himself regardless of how successful he is. He also knows that this is a never-ending process and that he must constantly search for new ideas and methods.

Maintain good health

The salesman, in addition to being concerned about his productivity, should also do whatever he can to achieve and maintain good health. Good physical and mental condition are important to any salesman who wants to be effective in his work. In maintaining good health the salesman should exercise regularly and watch his weight—particularly after 35 or 40 years of age, when a decrease in physical activity and a rich diet often lead to a gain in weight. The excess fat is put on at the expense of muscle and simultaneously puts a greater strain on the heart. A diet heavy in saturated fats along with insufficient exercise is often cited as the cause of cholesterol deposits in the blood which lead to atherosclerosis and heart attacks. Therefore, the salesman should exercise regularly and watch his diet so as to maintain a weight which is appropriate for his particular age and height.

Taking time out to relax or vacation is also necessary for maintaining good health. Periodic relief from everyday tensions helps to restore the joy of living. It is equally important to get a proper amount of rest each night, the amount required varying with the individual. Some people can get by with 6 or 7 hours of sleep, others need 8, and some may require 9 or 10 or even more. In any case, if a person is to do a full day's work and is to be effective in what he is doing, he must be well rested and have the necessary energy to do it.

The "self-managed" salesman will also have a physical checkup at regular intervals and will promptly respond to symptoms by seeking medical help. Some people foolishly delay attending to an ailment, thinking it is nothing serious and that it will eventually disappear. This might be true in some cases, but generally even minor ailments should be attended to promptly. "An ounce of prevention is worth a pound of cure," and your personal health is too valuable a commodity with which to gamble.

As mentioned in Chapter 2, the salesman should be optimistic and have the right mental attitude about his work and life in general. His state of mind will have a definite effect upon his mental and physical condition. Happiness and the right mental attitude are vital ingredients for maintaining good health.

Finally, the salesman should avoid smoking and excessive drinking. Current research has linked smoking with heart disease and lung cancer. As for drinking, it is an acceptable and enjoyable social custom but should be done in moderation. Nor should a man drink or use drugs to escape reality or to drown his troubles. This will only compound his problems and result in lost time, poor work performance, strained family relations, and deterioration of his health.

True or false?

_____ 1. A salesman should keep two sets of records—one for customers and another for prospects.

_____ 2. Salesmen should participate in community activities in their off-the-job time but should limit the time devoted to such activities.

_____ 3. Salesmen need not spend much time in self-analysis of their effectiveness because the company does it periodically for them.

_____ 4. Successful salesmen work hard day and night and take few breaks or vacations.

Now turn to Answer Frame 4¹⁴ on page 80 to check your answers.

Answer frame 4¹⁴

1. True. The information needed about customers and prospects normally includes: name, address, and phone number; dates of visits; amount and type of sale achieved, if any; problems, if any; points emphasized on call; and other miscellaneous items.
2. True. A salesman is part of the community and should take an active part in its activities such as the P.T.A., Kiwanis, and his church. But he should not participate to the extent that it prevents him from spending adequate time on his job or with his family.
3. False. In order to improve his performance, a salesman should periodically review himself on a subjective basis to test his product knowledge, his image, his presentation, and his relationship with his clients.
4. False. Taking time out to relax or vacation is necessary for good health. A tired salesman is not a sharp salesman.

If you missed any of the above, you should restudy Frame 4¹⁴ before beginning Chapter 15 below.

chapter 15

RETAIL SELLING

Frame 1¹⁵

Retail selling differs from other types of selling mainly in that it takes place in a store to which the prospect comes. He often arrives with some preconceived ideas regarding what he wants, and he is usually closer to buying than are prospects when they are approached by the outside salesman. The store name, advertising, special sales, eye-catching displays, and pleasant surroundings create a favorable environment that helps the salesman to sell. The retail salesman generally sells in an atmosphere where there is less noise, fewer interruptions, and less time pressure. Also, in retail selling the salesman generally handles more products than does a typical outside sales-

man. In addition, the retail salesman normally does not have the degree of freedom and independence that an outside salesman has in terms of deciding when, where, how, and to whom he will sell. Another difference is that retail selling tends to place more emphasis on buying versus selling. Prospects usually expect more selling effort by an outside salesman, but a retail salesman must be more low keyed and may even deliberately avoid too much emphasis on selling. His prospects have already made up their minds to a great extent, and they therefore tend to resist or resent too much emphasis on salesmanship per se.

Basic processes and purposes

The processes in retail selling normally follow these seven steps:

1. The customer is approached with a greeting or question.
2. The salesman determines what the prospect needs or wants.
3. Merchandise is selected in accordance with the prospect's requests; then it is shown, explained, and demonstrated with its benefits emphasized.
4. Questions and objections are answered and handled.
5. A close is attempted, along with suggestion selling if it is appropriate.
6. The merchandise is wrapped, then payment is received or the merchandise is charged.
7. Last, the customer is assured that he has made a wise purchase, is thanked for his patronage, is given additional advice or free items, is invited to come back again, and encouraged to contact the salesman if there are any additional questions or problems.

The major purpose of the sale is to *serve and satisfy* the customer. The retail salesman has also been trained to act as if the customer is always right and to accept the fact that the buyer should never be sold something he does not need. This objective is often expressed as "selling products that won't come back to customers who will." Retail selling should also be distinguished from "clerking," where little or no selling is done. The clerk's duties simply are to show the prospect where the merchandise is located, to wrap it if he decides to buy, and to receive payment or make out a charge sale. Hence, there is a big difference between clerking and selling. Clerking is less involved and largely mechanical, whereas, selling is more complex and requires infinitely more skill.

Approaching the retail customer

The three types of openings which are generally used in retail selling are the *greeting* or *comment* approach, the *service* approach, and the *merchandise* approach.

The greeting or comment approach is often expressed in such words as:

"Good morning, afternoon, or evening."
"It certainly is a nice day, isn't it?"
"It was just announced that our local team won the district championship."
"It was just announced that the tornado alert has been lifted."
"How do you do, Sir?"

The service approach is more direct and is used when saying:

"May I help you?"
"Are you being served?"
"Good afternoon, may I be of assistance?"

Service questions to avoid are:

"Are you looking for something?"
"Anything today?"
"Something for you today?"
"What'll you have?"

When the prospect is looking at or handling the merchandise, the salesman can use a merchandise approach. It can be expressed by saying:

"That shirt is on special sale this week and has been marked down from $7.95 to $4.95."
"That sports coat is the one which we recently advertised."
"Those shoes were just received on a special shipment from England."
"That is the latest color which is featured in the new spring fashions."
"That panelling is the best we have. It is a half an inch thick."
"That tie is made of pure silk."

In using the merchandise approach, the salesman should refer to major features of the product which he is reasonably certain will be of interest to the prospect. He should also mention only one or two points; otherwise the approach will be too long and may smack of high-pressure selling.

The manner in which the approach is made is more important than the particular approach itself. The customer should always be approached in a sincere and friendly manner. He looks upon himself as a guest who has been invited to the store and expects the salesman to be pleased with his visit. The salesman is therefore a host and should be polite and courteous when greeting his guests, the customers. It is especially important for the salesman to remember this if he is doing something when the customer arrives. In such cases, he may neglect the customer, or worse yet, appear annoyed. Idle gossiping or visiting with other salespeople in the presence of a customer is also bad. It costs money to attract customers to a store, and such behavior only drives them away. The salesman should also be careful not to overdo the approach. It is appropriate to call a man "Sir," but inappropriate to address a woman as "Madam," which is altogether too affected. The salesman should also avoid false flattery and "dripping honey" compliments. Instead, he should be sincere, friendly, businesslike, and polite.

Methods for increasing retail sales

The more important means for being productive in selling are to have the right attitude about selling, to know your merchandise, know how to analyze customer needs and wants, know how to organize the presentation, be skillful in persuad-

ing and closing, and know how to follow through and develop a customer following. However, sales can also be increased through *suggestion selling, selling multiple or larger units,* and *"trading up."*

Suggestion selling is selling additional merchandise which is related to the original purchase. For example, after selling a suit, the salesman often suggests a shirt or tie to go with it. Or after selling a pair of shoes, it is often appropriate to suggest a pair of socks, shoe polish, or extra laces. The suggested item normally should be lower in price and related to the original purchase. It is also good practice to display or show the related item with the original one during the presentation, rather than waiting to suggest it at the end of the first sale. In this way the second item often suggests itself without the salesman having to mention it. In suggesting related items, the salesman usually should not suggest more than one or two items because mentioning more than this number might be interpreted as high-pressure selling.

Label each of the following statements as true or false.

_____ 1. Retail salesmen place more emphasis on helping the customer to buy than selling the customer new ideas.

_____ 2. A retail salesman is the same as a retail clerk.

_____ 3. The approach of a retail salesman varies, but it must always be done in a sincere and friendly manner.

_____ 4. "Suggestion selling" will most likely be interpreted as high-pressure selling and is therefore not recommended.

Now turn to Answer Frame 1[15] on page 84 to check your answers.

Frame 2[15]

Methods for increasing retail sales (continued)

Occasionally, unrelated items may be suggested to customers. There may be no relationship between a rake and a gallon of paint; but if the store is having an unusual closeout sale on paint at a bargain price, the salesman might be doing the customer a service by mentioning it. For example, he might say something like this: "If you are interested in paint, our paint department is having a special closeout sale this week and offering it for one-half its original price." Chances are the

customer will indicate he has no need for paint, but sometimes the unrelated item suggested may be something he is definitely interested in purchasing.

Sales may also be increased by selling more than one unit of the same product, or by selling it in larger amounts. For example, the salesman might say, "These shrubs are $1.95 each or three for $5." Or the same idea can be expressed by saying, "These shrubs are $1.95 each. However, if two are purchased, you may purchase a third one for one-half its regular price." Or in the case of selling milk, the salesman can suggest buying more by saying, "Our milk is 35 cents a quart, 65 cents a half gallon, or $1.20 for a full gallon." Attempts to sell more than one unit or in larger quantities are especially appropriate for products which are frequently purchased or those which are commonly bought in lots of more than one. The salesman should not look upon this type of selling as being high pressure, for in many cases the customer wishes to be informed about price differentials which can save him money.

Sales can also be increased by using *alternative choice questions* rather than asking the prospect if he wishes to make a single purchase. For example, it is better to say, "Do you wish to purchase one or two pairs?" rather than saying, "Do you wish to purchase a pair?" Another example would be, "May I fill it up, Sir?" rather than saying, "How many gallons do you wish to purchase, sir?"

"Trading up" refers to suggesting that the customer buy a better-quality and higher-priced item than he originally intended to purchase. Great care should be exercised in using this type of suggestion because not all prospects can afford, nor do they need, the better and most costly merchandise. An illustration of this would be the average homeowner who is interested in purchasing a circular saw. One has roller bearings and is priced at $29.95 and the other has ball bearings and is priced at $59.95. Actually, the $29.95 saw with roller bearings is satisfactory for him because he normally uses a saw no more than 10 or 12 times a year. Moreover, the total amount of cutting time usually is only two or three hours each time he uses it. On the other hand, the roller bearing saw priced at $59.95 is designed for heavy duty use. Professional carpenters and contractors need such a saw because they use it from two to four hours every day. Thus, the price level of the product should be geared to what the prospect *needs* as well as what he *can afford*. If the salesman at the beginning of sale does not know the prospect's needs or what he can afford, it is usually advisable to start with the *middle* price, then go to the *higher* price if possible, and drop to the *lower* price if necessary.

It is also poor procedure to show the prospect too many products at once. To show him a great array of products may only confuse him and cause him to delay the purchase. Therefore, when the prospect indicates that he is not happy with one product, it should be removed so full attention can be devoted to the next product.

Know your merchandise

A major criticism frequently directed at the retail salesman is that he does not know enough about his merchandise. Too often he is unable to answer basic questions about his product and his knowledge is limited to only knowing its different sizes or models and the different prices of each. This is most unfortunate because customers expect the salesman to know his merchandise and to be able to answer their questions. It is therefore important for him to know the *major selling points* of his product, the *benefits* it offers to the customer, and *how it compares* with other similar products.

For example, in selling a hardwood picture frame, he should have the information suggested in Figure 15–1.

In selling a silk tie the points shown in Figure 15–2 should be mentioned.

A hardwood picture frame and a silk tie are relatively simple, and products such as suits, appliances, and furniture, have many more features to which the salesman can refer. For example, in selling a sports coat, reference can be made to the following points:

The type of material it is made of and in what quantities.
How it is woven.
How it is dyed.
How it is finished.
The stitching on the collar and the lining underneath.
The stitching on the lapel.
The kind and number of buttons on the sleeves.
The buttonholes, which are sewn with strong nylon.
The two side pockets, which are stitched and fully lined inside with an extra built-in coin pocket.
The stitched vents in back of the coat.
The inside lining and the material of which it is made.

Answer frame 1[15]

1. True. A retail salesman must be low keyed and deliberately avoid too much emphasis on selling. His prospects have already made up their minds to a great extent and tend to resist too much emphasis on salesmanship.

2. False. A clerk tells the prospect where merchandise is located, wraps desired merchandise, and receives payment. Retail selling is more complex and requires more skill in satisfying customer needs.

3. True. Retail salesmen may use the greeting, question, or merchandise approach, but the manner in which the approach is made is more important than the particular approach itself.

4. False. As long as only one or two items are suggested, this is an effective method of increasing sales. Suggestion selling is selling additional merchandise which is related to the original purchase such as a tie with a suit. Often a suggestion of complementary items is gratefully received rather than interpreted as high-pressure selling.

If you missed any of the above, you should reread Frame 1[15] before turning to Frame 2[15] on page 82.

Frame 2[15] continued

FIGURE 15–1

Selling points	Benefits	Comparison
Made of selected hardwoods.	Attractive grain patterns.	Some frames are plain or covered with paper to look like hardwoods.
The corners are tightly stapled and glued.	A stronger frame will not come apart. Also, there are no unsightly corner joints.	Some are just loosely nailed and come apart easily.
The edges of the frame are ridged and routed.	Makes it more attractive and decorative.	Some are just plain.

FIGURE 15–2

Selling points	Benefits	Comparison
Made of pure silk.	Silk colors beautifully and has a rich, lustrous appearance. It also has a soft, luxurious feel. (Have customer actually feel it.) Silk holds its knot. (This feature should also be demonstrated.)	Some ties are made of inexpensive rayon which has a harsher color and feel.
Yarn dyed.	Each individual yarn is dyed, and the fabric therefore holds its colors better and is more uniformly colored.	Some colors are just printed on the finished fabric.

The salesman who refers to such features distinguishes himself from the average salesman and is able to give a more informative and convincing presentation. It is surprising how much valuable information can be obtained by reading the tags which are attached to the merchandise, asking the buyer and other salesmen questions, reading advertisements, and referring to product booklets and manuals. Effort and study on the salesman's part to increase his knowledge of his stock will improve his performance and make him a more successful salesman.

The store

In addition to knowing his merchandise, the salesman needs to know certain things about the store. He should know something about its history, growth, and development; who its major officers are; what type of products and services the store carries, and where the various departments are located. He should also know the store's policies and procedures relating to delivery, credit, layaway sales, handling complaints, and making adjustments and refunds. Furthermore, he should know what items are being advertised, when, and in which media; as well as which items are marked down and on special display. How often have you gone into a store and asked a salesman for information or instructions only to have him reply that he didn't know anything about it? Such a response makes the salesman look foolish and also projects a poor image for the store. He should therefore be reasonably well informed about general store matters, and such information can easily be obtained from his immediate supervisor, the personnel office, company booklets and brochures, from other salespeople, and by reading the store's daily advertising.

True or false?

_____ 1. Suggestion selling is limited to items which naturally are purchased with the primary selection.

_____ 2. It is always a good idea to trade up a prospect to a higher-priced item because the quality is usually better.

_____ 3. A retail salesman should know more about a product than its major selling points.

_____ 4. A retail salesman must be thoroughly familiar with the store, its policies, merchandise, and so on, in order to do an effective job.

Now turn to Answer Frame 2¹⁵ on page 86 to check your answers.

Frame 3¹⁵

Substitution selling

The retail salesman, more frequently than the outside salesman, will find it necessary to suggest items other than the one requested by the customer—to practice substitution selling. In some cases, the store will not have the item which is requested by the customer; and in others it has the item requested, but the customer's choice may be inappropriate.

If the store *does not have* the item requested by the customer, the salesman should immediately tell him so and refrain from criticizing the requested item or aggressively attempting to sell him something else. Instead, he should say something like this: "I'm sorry, but we don't carry that particular brand or product. However, I'll be happy to show you what we have." If the store has a product which is reasonably close to being what the customer wants, the salesman should show it to the customer and put it in his hands for inspection. He should also emphasize its major selling points and refrain from referring to it as a substitute.

When the store *has the item* requested, but it may be inappropriate for the customer, the salesman should follow these procedures. Show the customer the product requested and briefly mention its major selling points. Then show it alongside the more appropriate choice and also mention its selling points, but at greater length. Often a simple comparison will result in the customer deciding for himself that the suggested product is a more appropriate purchase. It is particularly important for the salesman to be tactful lest he offend the customer. Under no circumstances should he say, "We have that product, but you really should consider something

Answer frame 2¹⁵

1. False. If the store is having an unusual closeout sale on some unrelated item, the salesman may be doing the customer a favor by mentioning it.
2. False. The price level of the product should be geared to what the prospect *needs* and *can afford*. Sometimes a lower-priced item is exactly what the customer should use.
3. True. It is important for a retail salesman to know a product's major selling points, but he must also know the *benefits* it offers to the customer and *how it compares* with similar products.
4. True. A retail salesman should know something about the store's history; its major officers; the kind of merchandise available; policies relating to credit, delivery, layaway, refunds, and other such services; and what items are being advertised. Such information helps the salesman to answer all of a customer's needs.

If you missed any of the above, you should restudy Frame 2¹⁵ before turning to Frame 3¹⁵ on page 85.

Frame 3¹⁵ continued

else." Even if the salesman is right, customers will usually take offense to such a statement and may even leave the store.

Suggesting another more appropriate product is relatively common in selling gift items and other products which one party may be buying for another. If the selection appears to be inappropriate, it is the salesman's responsibility to make an effort to switch the customer to a more suitable purchase. For generally, if an unwise purchase is made, the merchandise is either returned or the customer ultimately becomes dissatisfied and may never return to the store again.

Express appreciation and give the customer something

After a sale has been successfully made and the transaction has been handled, the salesman should do five more things:

1. Assure him that he has made a wise purchase.
2. Actually give him something or give him some additional advice.
3. Thank the customer for his patronage.
4. Invite him to return again.
5. And tell him to call or come in if he has any further questions or problems.

For example, after selling a pair of shoes the salesman might say something like this: "You're going to like those shoes, Mr. Jones, because they'll wear like iron and you'll find them to be very comfortable. They might be a little tight to put on at first so I would like to give you this shoe horn. We greatly appreciate your business and please come back again. And if you have any further questions or problems, don't hesitate to contact us. It's been a pleasure serving you, Mr. Jones, and we'll see you again. Thank you."

Another example might be as follows in selling several gallons of paint: "You're going to enjoy working with this paint because it's so easy to apply. It will also outlast anything else on the market. Here are some sticks to stir it, and also a booklet with some helpful hints on painting. Thank you for your purchase, Mr. Jones, and please come back again. And if you have any further questions, don't hesitate to give us a call."

Sometimes customers will be undecided about the wisdom of their purchase. Or after they get home, they ask questions and begin to compare their product with others. Worse yet, sometimes other people will criticize the product which may cause the customer to become dissatisfied with his purchase. Consequently, he should be assured at the end of the sale that he has made a wise purchase and given some reasons to support this conclusion. Customers also want to be appreciated, so the salesman should thank them for their business. When the salesman offers additional help and gives him something *after* the sale is over, it shows that the salesman is genuinely interested in serving the customer to the fullest extent. He not only sells the merchandise, but he also develops a pleased and satisfied customer who will return to purchase from him again.

Handling different types of customers

No two customers are the same. There are many ways to classify them, for example, according to age, sex, level of education, occupation, health, marital status, income, and religion. They will have different attitudes, habits, and personalities. All of these factors make selling extremely challenging. One of the main responsibilities of the salesman is to analyze the type of person he is serving and to structure his presentation accordingly.

True or false?

_____ 1. If a retail store is out of a particular item, the salesman should disparage the item requested and suggest a substitute.

_____ 2. Even if the salesman feels that an item requested by a customer is inappropriate, he should not try to switch him to something else.

_____ 3. Retail salesmen should always end the sale by assuring the customer that he made a wise purchase, thanking him for his patronage, and inviting him to return again and to call if he has any questions.

_____ 4. A retail salesman must deal with a variety of people and must learn to evaluate the type of person he is serving and to structure his presentation accordingly.

Now turn to Answer Frame 3[15] on page 88 to check your answers.

Frame 4[15]

Some of the common customer types, with suggestions for selling them, are described in the following paragraphs.

Just-looking type. This customer wants to look at the merchandise on his own and may start to leave if he is approached. Therefore, he should be left alone. The salesman should also welcome him to look around and indicate that he will be nearby if the customer wishes assistance.

Hurried type. This customer is nervous and impatient; this indicates that he has little time or is in a hurry. Show him exactly what he is interested in, emphasize only a few major selling points, and be as brief as possible. Also, minimize interruptions, for he will often quickly leave if the salesman momentarily attends to something else.

Uncertain type. This person is undecided, wavers from one product to another, and usually seeks answers to several questions from a companion or the salesman. In handling this customer, the salesman should be patient, watch for signs of interest to follow up on, and make appropriate suggestions. He should also avoid long lags or leaving the customer alone.

Confused type. This customer often buys merchandise about which he knows little or nothing. He may be old, a foreigner, or a child. The salesman should put him at ease, be friendly and informal, determine his needs, and supply him with pertinent information in simple language. He should also refrain from asking too many questions for this may further confuse the customer.

Know-it-all type. The "know-it-all" is cocky, arrogant, makes a point of displaying his own knowledge about the merchandise, and frequently contradicts or questions salesman's statements. The salesman should attempt to disarm such a customer by being friendly and welcoming his comments. He should avoid arguing or disagreeing with the customer, try to utilize the customer's own comments to sell him, and offer to call the department manager for additional information.

Talkative type. This person enjoys talking about everything and anything. If left un-

Answer frame 3¹⁵

1. False. A salesman should not criticize an item that has been requested nor should he refer to a replacement item as a substitute. He should emphasize the positive points of his store's merchandise and demonstrate how it will solve the customer's needs.
2. False. It is a salesman's responsibility to prevent a customer from making a wrong choice; otherwise, the customer will probably be dissatisfied and will want to return the merchandise.
3. True. Some customers are unsure about a purchase. A salesman can minimize such worries by assuring the customer that the merchandise is appropriate by offering to answer any questions that may arise, and giving the customer the feeling that he welcomes his patronage.
4. True. Retail customers vary in age, sex, level of education, occupation, income, and other factors which make it necessary for the salesman to adapt his presentation to the type of person he is serving.

If you missed any of the above, you should restudy Frame 3¹⁵ before turning to Frame 4¹⁵ on page 87.

Frame 4¹⁵ continued

checked, he may leave without buying. The salesman should be polite, listen for a few moments, and then refer back to the merchandise, thus maintaining control of the presentation. The salesman should avoid being sidetracked and getting into a discussion of the customer's or his own personal affairs.

Quiet type. Occasionally there is a customer who says little or nothing, or he fails to respond to questions. The common procedures for handling him are to ask questions that can be answered with a "yes," get him involved by demonstrating and putting the merchandise in his hands, and repeat selling points in different words. The salesman should not repeat himself in louder tones, implying that the customer can't hear, and also should avoid awkward pauses.

Easily distracted type. This person has something else on his mind or is easily distracted by an unruly child or outside noises. In handling him, the salesman should attempt to eliminate the distraction if possible. He should also concentrate on the main selling points, be alert and peppy in order to maintain the customer's interest, and try to get his attention by asking questions and putting the merchandise in his hands.

Think-it-over type. This type of customer tends to put off buying decisions by saying he wants to "think it over." In handling this sort of person, the salesman should avoid being high pressure, but at the same time he should ask questions and refer to major selling points, particularly those which are of key interest to the customer. Sometimes it is appropriate to ask him what additional points or questions he wishes to have explained. However, the salesman should avoid doing this if he thinks it will give the impression of being high pressure.

Argumentative type. This person has a "chip on his shoulder," wants to argue, makes unreasonable demands, and refuses to be pleased. The salesman should let him do most of the talking to "get it off his chest" and should be courteous, polite, cool and calm. He should tactfully ask questions and attempt to show how the product will fulfill the customer's needs or solve his problems.

True or false?

_____ 1. A retail customer who is "just looking" should be given as much assistance as possible in order to help him find something he likes.

_____ 2. A retail customer who is in a hurry should be treated the same as all other customers in order to be fair.

_____ 3. The "know-it-all" type of customer should be deflated by arguing with him to show your superior knowledge.

_____ 4. If a customer wants to think it over, the salesman should avoid being high pressure, but at the same time ask questions and refer to major selling points.

Now turn to Answer Frame 4¹⁵ on page 90 to check your answers.

Frame 5¹⁵

Handling more than one customer

Occasionally the salesman will be required to handle more than one customer at a time. This creates a problem, because all the customers will want attention. The first customer, however, should receive priority. If the salesman turns to a second customer and serves him, the first customer will feel neglected. On the other hand, the second customer or customers will not want to be kept waiting or to be totally ignored. In such cases the salesman can say, "I'll be with you in a few moments. . . ."

At times, especially if a second customer knows what he wants or has the merchandise in his hands and is waiting to pay for it, the salesman can momentarily excuse himself from the first customer and promptly return to him after taking care of the second customer. It is also possible sometimes for the salesman to give the second customer something to look at while he is serving the first customer. It may even be possible to serve several customers simultaneously, especially when selling such products as shoes, clothing, furniture, and similar products where the customer likes to look and closely examine the goods. In such instances the salesman starts off with the first customer and gives him merchandise to examine. Then he proceeds to serve additional customers by doing the same thing with them, and returns to each of them throughout different phases of the sales process.

When a salesman sells to a customer who is accompanied by another person—a husband, wife, son, daughter, or friend—these persons should not be ignored by the salesman. The recommended approach is to stay neutral or to determine which party has the stronger influence in deciding the purchase and to gear the presentation mainly to that person. However, in any case where there is disagreement among customers on what to buy, the salesman should recommend the merchandise which he sincerely believes to be the appropriate choice.

Handling complaints

Customers will often return with complaints about the product resulting from improper use on their part or because of faulty merchandise. In either case, it is the salesman's job to receive the complaint and to handle it in a manner that will satisfy the customer. The first thing he should do when approached by a dissatisfied customer is to thank him for bringing the matter to his attention. He lets the customer know that he cares and that the store stands behind its products. Next, the salesman listens and determines the cause of the customer's grievance. He doesn't interrupt or correct him. He lets the dissatisfied customer tell the complete story and gets all the information relating to what happened, when, where, and under what circumstances. Then he either asks the customer what can be done to correct the problem, or mentions specific alternatives for solving it. And finally, he takes the necessary steps to correct the problem on the spot, or follows up within a few days with additional information or other means for solving it. He handles the matter as promptly as possible and follows through to make certain that what was promised is being done. There is nothing more annoying to a customer than to be told that his complaint will be attended to, and then for the salesman to forget all about it. Such action is deplorable, and a salesman should never make promises which he cannot or does not intend to fulfill.

Sometimes a problem is caused by another

Answer frame 4¹⁵

1. False. "Just-looking" customers want to look at merchandise on their own and often start to leave if approached. Therefore, they should be left alone.
2. False. A customer who is in a hurry should be shown exactly what he wants, only a few selling points should be mentioned, and interruptions should be minimized.
3. False. A salesman should disarm "know-it-alls" by being friendly to them and welcoming their comments.
4. True. "Think-it-over" types should be asked questions and given major selling points, but not if this gives the impression of high pressure selling.

If you missed any of the above, you should restudy Frame 4¹⁵ before turning to Frame 5¹⁵ on page 89.

Frame 5¹⁵ continued

department in the store, and the salesman is tempted to criticize that department in the presence of the customer. Such criticisms, however, should be avoided because they only result in projecting a poor image for the store. For example, if the problem was caused by late or slow delivery the salesman should not say, "We're always having problems with our drivers, and they just can't remember when the merchandise is supposed to be delivered." Instead, he should say something like this: "Our drivers generally deliver on time, and I certainly will call this matter to their attention."

Usually the single most important cause for customer dissatisfaction stems from poor selling. Either the product was not right for the customer or the salesman did a poor job in telling him how to use or operate it. Hence, a customer should never be sold a product he doesn't need, and the salesman must also make certain that the buyer understands how to use it properly.

Handling returns

Sales returns can range from 5 to 15 percent or more of total sales volume. They reduce commissions and profits and are a common problem in retail selling. Some reasons why customers return goods are as follows:

a) An item may be defective in material or workmanship.
b) An item may be damaged or broken in delivery or returned because it was delivered too late.
c) Sometimes there is a mistake or misunderstanding regarding the quality and/or price of the merchandise.
d) High-pressure selling and letting the customer buy something which is not appropriate for him results in a high rate of returns.
e) A poorly informed or indifferent salesman can also cause many returns.
f) Occasionally the customer will see something else which he prefers over the item he has purchased.
g) Sometimes goods are returned because unacceptable merchandise was substituted for what the customer ordered.
h) Frequently the customer will overorder or request the wrong product.

Whatever the cause, it is the salesman's responsibility to attempt to control and reduce returns. A high rate of returns hurts everyone, reflects unfavorably on the store, and results in lower profits. For the customer it is often embarrassing or annoying to return goods. And the salesman loses, too, for handling returns can reduce his earnings and takes him away from serving other customers. In addition, it should be remembered that a liberal return policy can also help to *increase* sales, for customers will not be afraid to buy if they know they may return the goods. Generally, the store's largest credit customers do the most returning. Hence, if the store has a generous policy on accepting returned goods, the salesman should emphasize this point. At the same time, it is his responsibility to do an effective job of selling so the goods will stay sold and not come back.

True or false?

_____ 1. When faced with two or more customers, a retail salesman always should wait on them in the order in which they arrive.

_____ 2. If a customer has friends or relatives with him, the salesman should not ignore them in his presentation.

_____ 3. Customers with complaints should be handled in a direct and forceful manner, especially when the salesman believes them to be wrong or unreasonable.

_____ 4. Policies on accepting returned goods can help to develop a positive store image as well as an unfavorable one.

Now turn to Answer Frame 5[15] on page 92 to check your answers.

chapter 16

INDUSTRIAL SELLING

Frame 1[16]

Because of the unique nature of industrial products or services and basic differences in marketing and buying habits, industrial selling represents another major division of selling.

Classification of industrial products

Industrial products are classified by McCarthy into five basic categories:*

1. *Major equipment or installations* including such items as production machines, lathes, presses, kilns, computers.

2. *Accessory equipment* which generally is shorter

* E. Jerome McCarthy, *Basic Marketing: A Managerial Approach* (4th ed.; Homewood, Ill.: Richard D. Irwin, Inc., 1971), chap. 13.

lived and less expensive than major equipment or installations. Such equipment includes portable drills, electric lift trucks, typewriters, filing cases, wheelbarrows, and other similar products.

3. *Basic raw materials* which are further processed and converted into finished, physical products. Examples of basic raw materials would be cotton, sugar cane, cattle, wheat, tobacco, lumber, and iron ore.

4. *Component parts and materials* which are similar to raw materials but undergo further processing and generally are finished and ready for assembly. Examples of such products are automobile batteries, tires, small motors, wire, paper, and textiles.

Answer frame 5¹⁵

1. False. The first customer should receive priority treatment, but sometimes other customers may be handled quickly and easily with little disruption. Each case must be decided according to the circumstances that prevail.
2. True. The recommended approach for a group is to stay neutral and determine which party has the strongest influence in deciding the purchase and gear the presentation to him.
3. False. A customer with a complaint should be thanked for calling attention to the problem, his whole story should be carefully listened to, he should be asked what remedy he seeks, and steps should be taken to solve the problem promptly.
4. True. A liberal return policy may help to *increase* sales because customers will not be afraid to buy if they know they may return the goods. A strict return policy will often result in creating dissatisfied customers.

If you missed any of the above, you should restudy Frame 5¹⁵ before beginning Chapter 16 on page 91.

Frame 1¹⁶ continued

5. *Supplies* which are used in the daily operation of a company but are not fabricated into a final, finished product. Examples would be paint, light bulbs, cleaning solvents, lubricating oils and greases, pencils, paper clips, coal, and fuel oil.

Characteristics of industrial selling

Buyers of industrial products usually are technically trained and buy for *business* firms, *institutions* such as schools or hospitals, and *governmental* agencies. They are highly specialized and generally buy on a rational basis with their three major buying motives being *quality*, *price*, and *service*. In most cases, the product or service must be custom tailored to exacting company requirements. Consequently, the buyer's needs and problems must be carefully surveyed by the salesman and specific selling programs should be prepared in advance of making the call.

Sales orders are generally of large size, are for a specified period of time, and usually are decided upon by several key persons such as the purchasing agent, the chief engineer, the plant manager, the president, the director of marketing, and others. Negotiations for buying are often extended over long periods of time and are usually in accordance with predetermined specifications which frequently involve competitive bidding.

Manufacturers of industrial products will generally have fewer salesmen than a manufacturer of consumer products. This occurs because industrial products are more selectively distributed versus consumer products which are mass marketed.

The industrial salesman will have fewer but larger accounts. His presentations will be more technical, longer, and involve seeing several persons rather than one in the same company. He must, therefore, be skillful in adapting his presentation to several different persons.

Industrial selling is also supported by less advertising and promotional assistance than the selling of consumer goods for it is considerably more technical and requires more emphasis on personal selling versus general advertising. As a result of these differences, the industrial salesman has more individual responsibility for selling.

Because of geographical restrictions, the industrial salesman is usually the only contact that the buyer has with the company he represents, and its image is determined almost solely by him. Such a relationship makes it necessary for the salesman to know more about company personnel and operating policies than is required of the salesman who sells consumer goods. The industrial salesman thus is more of a "consulting specialist" in comparison with other types of salesmen.

The channels of distribution in industrial markets are usually shorter, and selling is generally direct from the manufacturer to the user. Industrial demand is also a *derived demand*. What this market purchases is dependent upon what happens in end markets. For example, the amount of ore a steel mill buys is largely determined by the end market demand for automobiles, appliances, and other products made of steel.

Another characteristic of industrial selling is that occasionally reciprocity will be a factor in the sale. *Reciprocity* is the practice of buying from a particular company because it buys from you. If the product is comparable or better than competitive products in terms of quality, service, and price, such a practice poses no problem. As a matter of fact, under such circumstances it is the only logical, ethical, and sensible thing to do. However, problems occur when there is pressure to buy an inferior product reciprocally. Purchasing agents as a group, however, are professional

and responsible persons, and generally they will not succumb to the pressures of undesirable reciprocity. Their job is to buy the best product at the lowest price, and in the majority of cases, this policy is followed.

It is also common practice for most companies to buy from more than one industrial salesman. The risks are usually too great for a company to depend entirely on one supplier. Occasionally even the best of suppliers is unable to deliver the goods as promised because of such unforeseeable events as a strike, a plant breakdown, an unexpected inventory shortage, and other similar problems. Buying from two suppliers also has the added advantage of making the situation competitive and keeping both sellers "on their toes."

Label each of the following statements as true or false.

_____ 1. Industrial products are those which become part of another product or are used in the manufacturing process.

_____ 2. Industrial buyers include institutions such as schools and hospitals, governmental agencies, and business firms.

_____ 3. Industrial buyers usually buy on the rational basis, and their major motives are quality, service, and price.

_____ 4. Most industrial buyers concentrate their purchases on one major supplier to get a better price.

Now turn to Answer Frame 1[16] on page 94 to check your answers.

Frame 2[16]

The industrial salesman's requirements and qualifications

Industrial selling differs in several respects from other types of selling, especially where products are sold to middlemen for resale or to ultimate consumers. One of the main differences is that the manufacturer of industrial products will generally have fewer salesmen than a manufacturer of consumer products. The industrial salesman will also have fewer accounts. However, each of his calls will be more technical, longer, and involve seeing several persons rather than one in the same company in order to secure the sale. He is also supported by less advertising and promotional assistance than the salesman of consumer goods. Consequently, the industrial sales-

man has more individual responsibility for selling. His success is greatly determined by his technical experience and his ability to precisely analyze the buyer's problems.

The industrial salesman must be skillful in adapting his presentation to several highly qualified persons, such as purchasing agents, sales managers, accountants, the plant manager, the chief engineer, the president of the company, and several others. Moreover, because of geographical restrictions, he is usually the only contact that the buyer has with the company he represents, and its image is, therefore, determined almost solely by him. Such a relationship makes it necessary for him to know more about company personnel, operating policies, and services than is required of the salesman who sells consumer goods. The in-

Answer frame 1¹⁶

1. True. Representative industrial products include heavy equipment, light equipment, raw materials, processed materials, and operating supplies.
2. True. Government agencies, business firms, and various institutions are classified as industrial buyers and usually place large orders which are decided upon by several key people and negotiated over a long period of time. This sometimes involves predetermined specifications and competitive bidding.
3. True. Industrial buyers are highly specialized and generally have a technical background, so their decisions are usually based on rational motives such as quality, price, and service.
4. False. It is a common practice to buy from more than one company because the risks of potential strikes, breakdowns, or other problems are usually too great to depend on one supplier.

If you missed any of the above, you should reread Frame 1¹⁶ before turning to Frame 2¹⁶ on page 93.

Frame 2¹⁶ continued

dustrial salesman also serves more as a "consulting specialist" in comparison with other types of salesmen. Work in this area, therefore, requires a person who has technical expertise, good analytical abilities, and one who can creatively approach different problems in the field.

True or false?

_____ 1. An industrial salesman will usually have fewer accounts and his calls will be more technical, longer, and will involve seeing more decision makers than the typical salesman of consumer products.

_____ 2. Because of geographical restrictions, an industrial salesman is often the only contact between the company and the buyer.

_____ 3. An industrial salesman serves as a "consulting specialist" to his customers.

_____ 4. An industrial salesman usually deals only with purchasing agents and should plan his presentation accordingly.

Now turn to Answer Frame 2¹⁶ on page 96 to check your answers.

Frame 3¹⁶

Industrial buying practices

The involvement of top management in buying decisions is quite common, particularly with large purchases and in smaller firms. The purchasing agent handles purchase orders and has considerable authority in the purchase of some items and less with others. For example, sales managers will often be involved in deciding on the quality of the product to be ordered, for its quality will influence the price to be charged and how successfully the finished product can be sold in the field. Others are also often involved in the decision. For instance, in the case of selling steel, the industrial salesman must work with and secure the approval of the designing engineers, the research department, the purchasing agent, production engineer, the sales manager, and others. Or in selling packaging material, he must clear the decision with the product planning department, the sales department, advertising, production, purchasing, the customer service department, shipping, and even the legal department. Hence, the industrial salesman must understand many different operations within the company. He is usually selling to a "management team" with varying backgrounds and interests. He is also faced with the problem of constant changes which occur in the company. Frequently, men are promoted or transferred, titles and duties change, and it is not uncommon for fewer than 50 percent of those involved in buying decisions to remain in the same job throughout the year.

As mentioned, the major buying motives of the purchasing agent are *quality, price,* and *service.* Quality refers to the suitability of the product or service. It must fulfill specific requirements if it is to be successfully marketed. For example, steel must have a certain hardness to be used in tools. Consequently, a product not meeting the required degree of hardness would not be acceptable. This is why industrial buying is geared to predetermined specifications, and any product falling below requirements is automatically rejected. Quality can also refer to how the buyer regards the salesman and the company he represents. Some salesmen and companies have a "quality" image while others do not.

Price is an important consideration in industrial selling, for the cost at which the material is bought will greatly influence the dollar volume of sales in the end market, as well as profits that will be made. The purchasing agent naturally attempts to purchase the *best* and *most* for the *least* amount of money. However, if the agent forces the seller to sell at an unprofitable price, it can often work against his own company's best interest. In such cases, the seller may be forced to "cut corners" by decreasing the quality or service he normally offers. Or he may simply stop selling to the purchasing agent and make it necessary for him to find a new source of supply. The old adage that "You get exactly what you pay for" certainly

applies to industrial buying, and the purchasing agent must therefore weigh the importance of price in relation to the quality and service it buys.

Service includes such things as dependable and prompt delivery. It would be a problem of major proportions if a buying firm's entire production line had to be closed down because the seller had failed to deliver the material as promised. Service also includes prompt attention to problems or breakdowns that might occur after the product has been sold, research assistance and advice, and satisfactorily handling product returns and adjustments.

The purchasing agent is also concerned with the reactions and preferences of the employees who use the product or service which he buys. Brand A may be more effective and easier for them to use than brand B. Another factor he might consider is the company's objective of making their product more marketable by using a material or part which is nationally advertised and has a high degree of consumer acceptance.

Purchasing agents are technically oriented and highly specialized in the products or services they buy. It is, therefore, easy to conclude that they buy strictly on the basis of reason and that emotions or subjective factors have little or no influence in their buying decisions. It is true that they apply specific and objective criteria in evaluating the products they buy. However, this does not mean that emotional factors are completely ruled out, particularly as prices become more competitive and product qualities become more similar. In such situations, company advertising and the personality of the salesman become increasingly more important for determining which product will be purchased.

Label each of the following statements as true or false.

_____ 1. Top management is often involved in industrial buying decisions, and industrial salesmen must be able to make presentations to these top-level corporate officers.

_____ 2. An industrial salesman often sells to a "management team" with varying backgrounds and interests, and he must adjust his presentation accordingly.

_____ 3. The only motive to buy for most purchasing agents is price.

_____ 4. Employee preference may be used as a selling point even if the product is higher priced.

Now turn to Answer Frame 3[16] on page 96 to check your answers.

Answer frame 2¹⁶

1. True. The industrial salesman has more individual responsibility for selling and he needs technical skills to call on fewer buyers with more complex problems.
2. True. An industrial salesman often is the sole determinant of his company's image because he is the only contact the buyer has with the company.
3. True. As a consulting specialist, an industrial salesman must have good analytical abilities and be able to creatively approach different problems in the field.
4. False. An industrial salesman must be skillful in understanding and adapting his presentation to sales managers, accountants, plant managers, chief engineers, company presidents, and others in addition to purchasing agents.

If you missed any of the above, you should restudy Frame 2¹⁶ before turning to Frame 3¹⁶ on page 94.

Answer frame 3¹⁶

1. True. Top management is often included in the decision-making process as are sales managers and others in the firm.
2. True. When selling to management teams, a salesman may face people he has never met before because of transfers, promotions, and so on. He must be able to adapt to these new people and vary his presentation accordingly.
3. False. Purchasing agents are concerned with quality and service as much as price and try to get the *best* and *most, when* they want it, at the *lowest* price.
4. True. Employees sometimes have definite preferences for products that are easier to use or are cleaner or safer. These are selling points which overshadow price and service considerations.

If you missed any of the above, you should reread Frame 3¹⁶ before turning to Frame 4¹⁶ below.

Frame 4¹⁶

Industrial sales presentations

The industrial salesman generally does not attempt to sell a product or service on the first call. Instead, his objective usually is to get permission to make a survey of the buyer's operation. If the buyer agrees, the salesman will often have additional personnel from the home office help in conducting the survey. This practice is especially common if the product is highly technical and involves several areas of specialization. The salesman will also work closely with personnel of the buying company. When the survey is finished, the salesman will prepare a formal report and present it to the purchasing agent and other interested parties. Many times it is presented to a group of people who serve as a formal buying committee.

In order to do an effective job, the industrial salesman must carefully prepare his presentation prior to giving it. He must know all phases of the buyer's operation, the needs and interests of all the persons to whom he will be talking, and how he proposes to decrease their costs and thus increase their profits by using his product. This is no simple task and it requires extensive preparation. All the benefits he mentions must be supported with specific facts, figures, charts, graphs, and other materials. He will often use samples, models, sketches, slides, films, and other aids to illustrate his points. He must be "razor sharp" during the presentation and be able to field questions from everyone. All can be lost if he becomes confused or is unable to answer key questions.

In addition, the salesman must gear his presentation to the specific interests of each person present, and at the same time make it of interest for the group as a whole. He should always identify the person who has the most authority in the group and attempt to involve him in the presentation in order to help influence the others.

Sometimes, however, the leader of the group may remain silent during the presentation. Then the salesman must involve those with less authority in such a manner as to convince the leader. In making his presentation, the salesman will often use other persons from his company to help explain certain points which require a high degree of expertise. Frequently, he will also be accompanied by members of top management, including the president and vice president, particularly if the sale might result in an unusually large order.

To be a successful industrial salesman requires considerable skill and training. Purchasing agents not only buy from him, but they also rely on him for information on new products, improvements, and new applications or uses. He also is a source of information on what other companies are doing. Purchasing agents expect the industrial salesman to help them with their problems. They do not want him to take up their valuable time with idle conversation or unnecessary visits. Therefore, he must carefully plan each call and design it to serve the buyer in some specific way.

In summary, the work of an industrial salesman is highly creative and challenging. It is also very rewarding work in terms of what is accomplished, the type of people with whom he works, and the money he earns.

Label each of the following statements **as** true or false.

_____ 1. Usually, the purpose of an industrial salesman's first call is to make a sales presentation.

_____ 2. It is a good idea to identify the person in the group who has the most authority and attempt to involve him in the sales presentation.

_____ 3. An industrial salesman will often bring other members of his firm to a sales presentation to give him expert support.

_____ 4. Most firms view industrial salesmen as helpful consultants and problem solvers rather than as representatives of a particular firm or interest.

Now turn to Answer Frame 4^{16} on page 98 to check your answers.

Answer frame 4¹⁶

1. False. The industrial salesman generally does not attempt to make a sale on his first call. Instead, his objective usually is to make a survey of the company's operation to determine what the buyers needs are.
2. True. This can have a great positive influence on others attending the meeting.
3. True. In making his presentation, an industrial salesman will often call upon experts from his firm, including the president and vice president.
4. True. An industrial salesman is often viewed as a consultant who is a source of information about what other companies are doing, new product developments, new applications of old products, and various problem-solving ideas. As such, he is a valuable help to the customer.

If you missed any of the above, you should reread Frame 4¹⁶ before beginning Chapter 17 below.

chapter 17

SALES MANAGEMENT

Frame 1¹⁷

Traditionally, sales management has been viewed as the management of such sales-related activities as recruiting and selecting a sales force and then training, evaluating, compensating, supervising, and motivating these salesmen. However, since around 1950, the responsibilities of the sales manager have been greatly expanded in many instances to include such related activities as product planning, pricing, sales forecasting, customer service, channel considerations, and advertising. As more and more firms become "marketing oriented" and with the increasing growth of consumerism, the sales manager of today is becoming more involved in the whole spectrum of marketing activites. Accordingly, his work is more complex and requires a higher degree of education and training.

Differences between sales management and other types of personnel management

Though related to personnel management, sales management warrants special attention in comparison with the management of other classes of business personnel (such as accountants, office workers, and those in finance) because the salesman's job is so different from other jobs within the company. This difference exists primarily because the salesman is in the public eye more than other types of workers. The impressions that consumers have of a particular company and its products are often formed by their contact with the salesman. Thus the salesman is an official representative of the firm. His work also differs from that of other workers in that he operates with a higher degree of freedom and independence; he has a great deal more freedom to determine his own productivity. In comparison with many other activities, the salesman's work requires self-initiative, creativity, and persistence; and these qualities in turn, require a higher degree of motivation.

The very nature of his work requires that the salesman possess more social poise. In many instances he will be selling to persons who have high social or corporate standing, and he must be able to identify with, and be accepted by, these people. Such acceptance requires a high degree of social intelligence not ordinarily required in other types of work.

In addition, the salesman is one of the few employees who is allowed to spend company funds. He is responsible for the amounts he will spend on travel, meals, lodging, and entertainment; and the expenses he incurs in these areas will greatly influence company costs and profits.

Finally, many selling jobs require considerable traveling and being away from home. Such circumstances, plus the fact that he will usually encounter a great deal of customer resistance, creates tensions and pressures that are absent in many other jobs. Because of these different circumstances and responsibilities, sales management demands special attention over and above that which management devotes to other types of business personnel.

Major responsibilities of the sales manager

The responsibilities of the sales manager will vary with the size and type of company, as well as with its corporate structure. Usually, however, his main responsibilities will be to supervise the sales force; to recruit, select, and train sales personnel; to manage the local sales office; to serve as the coordinating link between top management and the sales force; and in some cases, to engage in personal selling. Also, to the degree that his company accepts the marketing concept, he will be involved in decisions related to product development, pricing, the "marketing mix," and others.

In supervising the sales force, the sales manager assigns sales territories, determines quotas, and decides how the salesmen will be compensated. He is also concerned about how the salesman allocates his time by types of customers and product lines. He attempts to secure maximum effectiveness by analyzing sales reports and suggesting work patterns. He must know how to motivate the salesman by utilizing various incentives and rewards. This is a persistent problem because salesmen usually work alone in the field and can easily become discouraged. These conditions make motivation a major responsibility of the sales manager for the salesman must continue to have a positive and determined attitude if he is to succeed. The sales manager must also evaluate the salesman's performance—usually by comparing his actual sales with a predetermined or expected standard. And in those cases where the salesman's performance is unsatisfactory, the sales manager must know how to analyze the salesman's problems and be able to make suggestions to help him.

In the recruiting, selection, and training of sales personnel, the sales manager is often aided by other persons. However, his policies will determine where and how persons will be recruited, the types of persons who will be selected, the methods that will be used in selecting them, and the type of program that will be developed to train them.

The sales manager's duties in managing the local office will vary greatly depending upon its size and functions. It may be operated by a single secretary, or in other cases by several secretaries, a bookkeeper or accountant, a service man, a janitor, a plant manager and his staff, a warehouseman, and other similar personnel. The sales manager alone will be responsible for managing the operation of a smaller office; but for a larger one, he usually will have to employ an assistant sales manager and maybe even an office manager. As manager of the local sales office, he is also frequently responsible for representing the company. In this role he is expected to participate in local community affairs, to contribute to charities, and to participate in various service organizations.

In his role as the coordinating link between top management and the sales force, the sales manager must serve as an intermediary. It is his job to communicate the policies of top management to the salesmen; and in like fashion, to communicate the needs and problems of the salesmen to top management. This is no simple task because he is often caught between two conflicting viewpoints. For example, top management is always interested in controlling and reducing expenses, while salesmen sometimes are more interested in increasing sales with less concern about the expenses involved in achieving them. Nevertheless, the sales manager must know how to secure the cooperation of both groups, for it is his responsibility to get the job done.

Label each of the following statements as true or false.

_____ 1. Since around 1950, the sales manager's responsibilities have been expanded in many companies to include product planning, pricing, customer service, channel considerations, and advertising.

_____ 2. The sales manager's job is no different from the management of other functional areas such as personnel, accounting, and finance.

_____ 3. One of the major responsibilities of the sales manager is to continually motivate the salesmen under him.

_____ 4. The duties of all sales managers are restricted to recruiting, selecting, and training sales personnel.

Now turn to Answer Frame 1[17] on page 102 to check your answers

Frame 2[17]

Should the sales manager also sell?

Whether or not the sales manager should also do personal selling is one of the most controversial questions concerning his responsibilities. Arguments in favor of his selling are that major accounts usually require the attention of senior personnel, such as a sales manager. It is also argued that it is logical for him to continue to handle the major accounts he served as a salesman. Furthermore, it is said that a sales manager cannot keep abreast of current problems in selling unless he himself continues to sell. Arguments against his selling are that it often puts him in competition with the salesmen under him while he has the advantage of picking the better accounts. Others contend that sales management and selling are two distinct functions, that each is a full-time job in itself, and that the two jobs should, therefore, be separated.

A key factor in these conflicting viewpoints is the fact that often the top salesmen are chosen for sales management positions. It cannot be disputed that demonstrated effectiveness in selling can be an important asset for a sales manager. However, it does not guarantee that he will be a good manager. As a matter of fact, such traits as aggressiveness and the desire to be independent, which are usually associated with successful selling, might turn out to be detrimental traits when applied to managing others.

In summary, many successful salesmen can become successful sales managers, but sales management requires the ability to plan and organize and to work *with* and *through* others. Studies also show that successful sales managers receive higher salaries as compared with persons in other types of work. Annual sales of a firm are commonly regarded as a measure of its success. In this sense, then, the sales manager has considerable visibility and is one of the most important persons in the company. Consequently, successful selling experience and work as a sales manager are two of the fastest steps to higher corporate positions.

Sales forecasting

The sales manager is usually responsible for making company sales forecasts, which are an estimate of the sales that will be made for a particular period of time, such as a season or a year. The sales forecast is one of the key factors in arriving at the overall company budget. It becomes the blueprint for company planning, and the productive requirements of all the other departments are carefully geared to it. Sales managers who make short-run forecasts are interested in seasonal matters or developments; those making long-run forecasts are interested in trends.

There are several different approaches to forecasting company sales. Representative methods are discussed in the following paragraphs.

Management consensus. A consensus of opinion of top company executives as to what sales will be provides a quick and easy method of forecasting. Such a forecast will be based on inputs from several sources rather than a single source. But forecasts arrived at by this method sometimes amount to nothing more than educated guesses. Many of the persons who participate in making the forecast may be poorly qualified. Also, the data relating to the market on which executives base their predictions may be highly inaccurate. Moreover, it is often difficult to break this type of forecast down into quotas.

Sales force summary. A forecast may be arrived at by using estimates secured first from the salesmen and then carried upward through the sales organization, each level accumulating data from the preceding one and passing on a forecast of estimated sales. The district manager makes his forecast based on inputs from the salesmen, then the regional and divisional managers make their estimates, and so the forecast moves upward to the highest marketing executive. Proponents of this method hold that the person who knows the market best is the salesman himself, the man who is in closest contact with the consumer. The procedure is more realistic than depending solely on the views at the top, because the persons participating in the forecast are also the ones to whom the quotas will be assigned. In addition, the weaknesses and dangers of one-man forecasts are avoided, and operating breakdowns of the forecast are relatively easy to make. Arguments against this method are that some salesmen will be too optimistic in their expectations, while others will be too pessimistic. It is argued that some will deliberately underestimate the market in order to get a smaller quota. Moreover, this method is quite time consuming, and some of the salesmen may resent having to participate. Finally, most salesmen are well informed about market conditions in their territories, but they may be poorly informed about economic conditions on a national level which could affect company sales.

User estimates. Some companies will make their forecast by asking their customers what and how much they plan to buy for a given period. Advantages of this method are that the forecast is based on the estimates provided by the users whose buying actions will actually determine sales. It also gives the company a more detailed and better understanding of the buyers' intentions. Arguments against this method are that it is difficult to employ in markets where there are many customers or in markets where they may be difficult to locate. Such a forecast assumes that the product user will be well informed and willing to participate. However, in actual practice some of the product users will be poorly informed and indifferent or reluctant about participating. This method also bases the forecast on estimates, which are subject to possible change. Finally, it requires considerable time and manpower to collect such information.

Using past and current sales as basis for prediction. This method recognizes that past sales and current sales can help to predict what the future sales will be. For example, the forecaster may expect favorable changes again next year which will increase sales volume by approximately 10 percent as compared with an increase of 9 percent for the current year and an increase of 8 percent in the past year. Relatively simple and easy to use, this method can help predict both for the short term and the long term. However, putting so much emphasis on past and current sales may prevent recognition of changes in conditions that can occur quickly.

Taking account of changing economic and social conditions. In companies where sufficient economic and statistical expertise is available, the sales forecast can be made to reflect those changing conditions in the overall economy or in the industry which could have an effect on the sales of the individual firm. Gross national product and extension of future trends can be used as a measure of the present and expected business prosperity. The sales forecaster must then interpret the effect the anticipated upsurge or recession will have on his firm's sales.

Changing patterns in population, too, can be

Answer frame 1¹⁷

1. True. As more firms become marketing oriented, sales managers become more involved in the whole spectrum of marketing activities.
2. False. Since salesmen are in the public eye, directly spend corporate funds, work with a relative degree of independence and self-motivation, and travel extensively, the job of managing them is much different from that of managing other workers.
3. True. A sales manager must know how to motivate salesmen by utilizing various incentives and rewards. Motivation is a major responsibility, because salesmen must continue to have positive and determined attitudes if they are to succeed.
4. False. Sales managers have many duties besides recruiting, selecting, and training such as managing the local sales office, coordinating top management and sales efforts, personal selling to select accounts, and managing activities such as territory allocation, quotas, compensation, and time allocation.

If you missed any of the above, you should reread Frame 1¹⁷ before turning to Frame 2¹⁷ on page 100.

Frame 2¹⁷ continued

taken into account. For example, when birthrate census data reveals a decline in the number of grade-school children in the population, this will serve to warn manufacturers of products designed for this age group to anticipate lower sales volume unless they can make up for the loss by increasing their market share.

Social patterns also must be watched for major changes in attitudes and tastes. When social attitudes discourage "keeping up with the Joneses," certain prestige products may suffer a loss in sales. A general shift away from materialistic values by the young would certainly have to be taken into account by those selling to the youth market.

Sales forecasting is an important function and determines the budgeting for all operations of the firm. Several methods are used depending upon the size of the company, the type of product or service it sells, and the number of customers involved. Each method has its respective advantages and disadvantages, and the specific methods chosen to make a forecast are one of the major responsibilities of the sales manager.

True or false?

_____ 1. One of the most controversial areas in sales management is whether or not the manager should be involved in personal selling.

_____ 2. The best salesmen always make the best managers.

_____ 3. Successful selling and work as a sales manager are two of the fastest steps to higher corporate positions.

_____ 4. Salesmen may or may not have a role in forecasting future sales.

_____ 5. Sales forecasts based on user's expectations or past sales have shortcomings which limit their effectiveness.

Now turn to Answer Frame 2¹⁷ on page 104 to check your answers.

Frame 3¹⁷

Sales quotas

Sales quotas are amounts in dollars or units that the salesman is expected to sell in a given territory for a given period of time. There are quotas for the salesman; for each area or territory; for product lines; for buyers; and quotas for a month, season, or year.

Quotas are very important in selling, for without them there can be no effective planning and control. They set up targets or goals for the salesman and his compensation, commissions and possibilities for promotion are directly related to them. Quotas help the sales manager to determine whether the salesman's territory is either too large or too small.

The most common type of sales quota assigns a *dollar volume of sales* to a specific geographical area or sales territory. The sales quota may also be related to profits, and in this case is called a *margin* and *profit* quota which encourages the salesman to sell the higher-profit items. Profits are also related to expenses, so there are *expense* quotas which make the salesman more conscious of costs. Usually, the salesman is told what his expense quota will be, and he is often given some type of reward if his expenses are lower than expected. Finally, there are *activity* quotas which are based on points rather than dollar or unit volume. Points are awarded for the number of calls made, the number of new customers gained, the number of presentations made, the degree of improvement, the number of point-of-purchase items installed, and other similar accomplishments. Activity quotas serve to motivate the salesman, and he is usually rewarded for his accomplishments in money or prizes.

In setting sales quotas in dollars, the sales manager will first study the sales potential in each area or territory. If the "sales force summary" method is used, he automatically has the estimates for each geographic unit. However, if the "management consensus" method is used, he has a total figure which must be broken down and assigned to the respective areas or territories. In order to do this, he must have a market index,

and one of the most widely used indexes of this sort is the *Sales Management's* annual "Survey of Buying Power."

In many instances, the forecast for a particular area or territory will automatically become the quota. For example, of a 100 percent dollar volume expected for a given territory, which three salesmen are assigned to cover, salesman A might be given a quota of 45 percent; salesman B, 30 percent; and salesman C, 25 percent. However, adjustments are sometimes necessary, and the sales manager may assign quotas of 50 percent, 35 percent, and 30 percent respectively for salesmen A, B, and C making a total of 115 percent. Such a quota is an "incentive quota" and is designed to both motivate and to insure that the original quota of 100 percent will be made. On the other hand, the quotas may be lowered because the sales manager knows that the salesmen involved are either too old or inexperienced to achieve a combined quota of 100 percent. In such a case, he might therefore set the quota at 90 percent for the territory and offer a bonus to those salesmen who achieve in excess of their respective quotas.

It should be noted that quotas should be practical and realistic. If they are too high or too low, they will usually fail to accomplish their objectives. They should also be understood and accepted by those who will be involved in achieving the quotas. Many sales managers encourage the participation of the salesmen in setting up quotas because it makes them better informed and more responsive. Quotas should also be fair and accurate and based on territorial potential rather than the sales manager's hunches or prejudices. Finally, there must be continuous follow-through on quotas, and the annual figure should be analyzed and reviewed each month.

True or false?

_____ 1. Sales quotas are very important in selling, for without them there can be no effective planning and control.

_____ 2. Dollar volume quotas are the only kind used by most sales forces.

_____ 3. In many instances, the forecast for a particular area or territory will automatically become the quota.

_____ 4. Quotas set very high will usually motivate salesmen to work harder and will result in effective sales stimulation.

Now turn to Answer Frame 3[17] on page 104 to check your answers.

Answer frame 2¹⁷

1. True. There are arguments for and against using managers as field salesmen, but it is difficult to be a good manager *and* a good salesman at the same time.
2. False. Demonstrated effectiveness in selling is an important asset for sales managers, but such traits as aggressiveness and a desire for independence, which are usually associated with successful selling, may be detrimental for managers.
3. True. The unique nature of sales management work makes it easier to evaluate performance and it is the only function which generates profits for the company.
4. True. Salesmen are often too optimistic or pessimistic in their expectations, but they often know more than managers about the marketplace. Managers are often more expert in analyzing sales trends. Therefore, salesmen are often used in sales forecasting, but sometimes this is the sole responsibility of management.
5. True. User's expectations and past sales both are based on data which may or may not be accurate in predicting future potential. Each forecasting method has its advantages and disadvantages, and choosing a method or combination of methods is a major responsibility of the sales manager.

If you missed any of the above, you should restudy Frame 2¹⁷ before turning to Frame 3¹⁷ on page 102.

Answer frame 3¹⁷

1. True. Sales quotas are applied to salesmen, territories, product lines, buyers, and periods of time to help the manager plan and control sales compensation, allocation of effort, and other sales functions.
2. False. Dollar volume quotas are the most common, but most sales forces also use margin and profit quotas, expense quotas, and activity quotas to get more control over these areas.
3. True. Although the forecast may become the quota, adjustments are often necessary because of the expertise and experience of salesmen, geographical differences, and other territory variables.
4. False. Quotas should be practical and realistic. Very high or very low quotas usually fail to accomplish their objectives.

If you missed any of the above, you should restudy Frame 3¹⁷ before turning to Frame 4¹⁷ below.

Frame 4¹⁷

Salesmen's compensation plans

Another important responsibility of the sales manager is to decide how the salesmen should be compensated. Basically, he wants to introduce a plan for compensating salesmen that will attract them in the first place, keep them in the company fold, and be sufficiently generous to motivate them to improve performance. At the same time, the plan must keep costs at a satisfactory level. Sales managers recognize that there are differences among salesmen, territories, products, and buyers. Accordingly, they want a plan that is flexible enough to apply to varying conditions. The plan adopted must also be in harmony with plans that are used for paying other company employees.

Salesmen, on the other hand, want a compensation plan which will give them a satisfactory income. Generally, they want two types of income: a steady income to cover basic living expenses and an added compensation which serves as an incentive and rewards them for certain levels of achievement. They also want a plan which is geared to those factors which they can control. This is sometimes difficult to achieve because market conditions may have changed and the plan under which the salesmen are paid is no longer appropriate. In addition, salesmen want a plan which is fair, which makes prompt payments, and one which is easy to understand and compute.

There are three basic compensation plans:[1] (1) straight salary, (2) straight incentive, and (3) salary plus incentive. Under the straight salary plan, the salesman is paid a fixed amount on a weekly or monthly basis. The advantages of this plan to the sales manager are that it gives him more direct control over the work of the salesmen. It is clear, specific, and relatively easy to administer. Payment on a regular and continuing basis gives the salesmen security and stability. It is also very appropriate for paying new employees or when introducing new products. Arguments against this plan are that it provides little incentive, and a greater burden is thrown on the sales manager for motivating the salesmen and supervising their work. Also, this plan sometimes is unfair—particularly when it rewards older and less efficient salesmen more than they deserve in comparison with the younger and more aggressive salesmen. The plan must also be reviewed frequently, for it can quickly become out of date.

Under the straight commission plan, the salesman is paid according to his performance or the amount he sells. The commission rate can either be fixed or paid on a sliding scale. Its principal merits are that it provides incentive and rewards the salesman in proportion to his efforts. The commission salesman also enjoys greater freedom in performing his work, and this plan generally attracts more capable salesmen. Its disadvantages are that the sales manager has less control over the salesman's activities. It is sometimes difficult to establish commission rates which are fair in all cases, and earnings of the salesman can fluctuate greatly, thereby giving him a feeling of insecurity and sometimes encouraging him to resort to high-pressure selling. Other problems are that house accounts (those accounts handled by the

company rather than a salesman) can cause resentment, and it is often difficult to divide a commission which is earned by two salesmen.

The salary-plus-commission plan is a compromise pattern which attempts to secure the advantages of both the straight salary and straight commission plans. Studies indicate that approximately 60 percent of the sales managers use this plan. There are four basic types of combination plans: (1) salary plus commission, (2) drawing account plus commission, (3) salary plus bonus, and (4) the point system.

Salary plus commission is the most common of the combination plans and is appropriate for salesmen who have to service the products they sell. Salaries under this plan can vary from 20 to 90 percent of the salesman's total earnings. Sometimes the salary figure is geared to the cost of living, and the commission is based on sales. Or the commission may be geared to sales volume over a given amount for a particular period of time. This plan involves more bookkeeping and therefore can be expensive to administer.

A drawing account is a system of payment whereby the salesman is paid in advance, and then he later repays the amount drawn from the commissions he earns. The amount is fixed, and he draws a given amount of money each week or month. Under a *guaranteed draw*, if the salesman's commissions are lower than the draw, he does not have to repay the draw. Under the *nonguaranteed draw*, however, the salesman is obligated to repay the amount advanced to him from future commissions. Drawing accounts tend to give the salesman greater security, but they also involve increased administrative work.

A bonus is a sum of money given to the salesman at the end of a given period for above average achievement or performance. One of the most common bonuses is the Christmas bonus. Because of the uncertainties involved with the bonus plan, it generally has less incentive value. However, it can be effectively used for rewarding salesmen on the basis of calls made, number of new accounts gained, increases in sales volume, degree of improvement, and other similar accomplishments.

In a company where activity quotas are set up, the point system may be used. Under this plan

---

[1] Adapted from C. A. Kirkpatrick, *Salesmanship* (4th ed.; Cincinnati, Ohio: Southwestern Publishing Co., 1966), pp. 559–64.

the sales manager rewards the salesman with points for various types of accomplishment. Generally, the salesman receives a given number of points for every $100 of sales volume, and the high-profit items in his line are assigned the highest points. Points may also be earned for the number of calls made, number of demonstrations, new accounts, and other similar accomplishments. Plus or credit points are the most common, but sometimes there can be negative or penalty points. If the salesman earns 800 points for a given month and the value of each point is one dollar, he receives a salary of $800. This system is rather complicated and difficult to administer and therefore is not widely used.

Compensation plans vary greatly, with the combination patterns being the most common. Regardless of the plan chosen, the sales manager will attempt to choose one which motivates the salesmen to maximum performance, and simultaneously one that is economical to administer.

Label each of the following statements as true or false.

_____ 1. Under a straight salary compensation plan, the salesman is paid according to his performance or the amount that he sells.

_____ 2. Straight commission salary plans provide considerable incentive and reward the salesman in proportion to his efforts.

_____ 3. The most common form of sales compensation is salary plus commission.

_____ 4. A "bonus" is merely another term for a "commission."

Now turn to Answer Frame 4[17] on page 108 to check your answers.

Frame 5[17]

Salesmen's expenses

In addition to obtaining effective selling performance, the sales manager must control salesmen's expenses if satisfactory profits are to be made. Personal selling expenses can amount to thousands of dollars each year per salesman and generally include transportation from town to town, local transportation, meals, tips, lodging, telephone and telegraph costs, mailing costs, laundry and valet expenses, and gifts and entertainment. Policies concerning the latter items vary widely, and there are differing opinions as to the extent of entertaining and gift giving that is effective, permissible, or ethical.

Sales expenses should be handled so as not to allow expense reimbursement to become a source of income. The salesman should be reimbursed only for the true amount of expenses he incurs. A good expense plan should also be clear, flexible, and economical to administer.

There are four basic patterns for paying expenses.[2] The first plan is where the *salesman pays all his own expenses.* For example, he may receive a total commission of 10 percent, of which 7 percent represents income or earnings, and the remaining 3 percent goes for expenses. This plan is relatively simple to administer, but it gives management little authority in controlling expenses and sometimes encourages salesmen "to skimp" on what they spend in order to increase their income. For these reasons this plan is not widely used.

A second plan for paying expenses is the *unlimited reimbursement* plan. Under this system there are no maximum limits, and the salesman is simply paid for the expenses he submits. This plan gives the sales manager little control over expenses and could lead to considerable padding and abuse. For this plan to work effectively with salesmen, they must be quite conscientious and responsible. A variation of this plan is where the salesman is required to submit an itemized report

---

[2] Ibid., pp. 565–67.

and each expense is separately examined and approved. This procedure is more time-consuming than the lump-sum version, but it gives the sales manager more control over expenses and also helps to reduce padding. This particular plan is very popular and is one of the most widely used plans for paying expenses.

A third pattern is the *limited reimbursement* plan. Under this system the salesman may be limited to a maximum total for a given period, such as a total of $20 per day or $100 per week. Or the total may be broken down, with maximum totals for each type of expense, so that there would be separate maximum totals for travel, for meals, lodging, and so on. This plan is a little difficult to administer, but it can be a good one if the maximum ceilings are realistic and adequate.

The fourth plan is the *flat expense allowance.* Under this system the salesman, instead of having a given percentage of his commission to cover expenses, is paid a flat dollar amount each day or week. It is a "per diem" method for handling expenses. It is clear and easy to administer. It is the sales manager's responsibility to see that the figure is no higher or lower than it should be. Sometimes the salesman will "skimp" in order to make money on his allowance, and there is always the problem of his eliminating certain activities altogether if he has exceeded his allowance for a given period.

Regardless of the plan used, expenses seem to be always increasing, and they have an important bearing on profits. Effective control of expenses is a constant challenge to the sales manager and will greatly determine his success or failure.

Characteristics of a successful sales manager

A sales manager must possess many skills and attitudes, which will vary by company and industry. The following list indicates some of the most important ones.

The sales manager must know how to get along and work effectively *with* and *through* other people.

He must be skillful in the art of communication and persuasion.

He must be able to motivate and lead others.

He must understand others and know how to help them.

He must know how to analyze and select new salesmen.

He must be competent in evaluating the performance of salesmen and know how to effectively train them.

He must know how to analyze and interpret varying types of data.

He must know how to plan and organize.

He must be capable of withstanding continual pressure and tension.

He must be imaginative and creative.

He must be flexible and capable of adapting to change.

If he expects to achieve high standards, he must be dedicated and professionally minded.

True or false?

_____ 1. Sales expenses should be handled so as not to allow expense reimbursement to become a source of income for the salesman.

_____ 2. When a salesman pays all his own expenses, he cannot be prevented from "skimping" on what he actually spends in order to increase his income.

_____ 3. Sales expenses are the concern of the salesmen and not a major concern for most sales managers.

_____ 4. All sales managers need the same skills and attitudes to be successful.

Now turn to Answer Frame 5^{17} on page 108 to check your answers.

Answer frame 4[17]

1. False. Under the straight salary plan, the salesman is paid a fixed amount on a weekly or monthly basis, and payment is not based on sales.
2. True. The straight commission plan provides much incentive for the salesman, but it is sometimes difficult to set fair commission rates, and management loses some control over the activities of the salesman.
3. True. A salary-plus-commission system compensates the salesman for selling and servicing customers. The terms of such a contract vary according to the company; its products, customers, and channels; and other such circumstances.
4. False. Bonuses differ from commissions in that they are not tied as directly to quantitative results. For instance, one might receive a Christmas bonus based on performance but not on a specific dollar volume.

If you missed any of the above, you should reread Frame 4[17] before turning to Frame 5[17] on page 106.

Answer frame 5[17]

1. True. Salesmen should neither make nor lose money when reimbursed for the expenses they incur. They should be reimbursed for the true amount they incur.
2. True. Letting a salesman pay all his own expenses is an easy plan to administer, but it gives management little authority in controlling expenses and sometime results in "skimping" on sales spending.
3. False. Expenses seem to be always increasing and have a direct effect on profits. Effective control of expenses is a constant challenge to sales managers and greatly determines their success or failure.
4. False. The skills and attitudes needed by a sales manager vary by company and industry, but he should be able to work with and through others; be a skillful communicator; be able to understand and motivate others; be able to analyze, plan, and organize; and be dedicated to his profession.

If you missed any of the above, you should restudy Frame 5[17] before beginning Chapter 18.

chapter 18

SELECTION AND TRAINING OF SALESMEN

Frame 1[18]

Effective selling begins with selecting persons who have the potential and desire to be successful salesmen and then giving them the proper training. Higher profit margins, increased competition, the high rate of turnover, and high costs of training have put more emphasis on better selection and training procedures. Present-day sales managers tend to reject the idea that "try out and fire" is a good enough basis for building a sales force. Most large companies, and even some smaller ones, now approve selecting and training of salesmen in an organized and scientific manner, using the tools provided by psychological testing and research.

Current methods used for selecting salesmen

The methods used for selecting salesmen will vary depending upon the type of product or service being sold, the size and objectives of the company, the conditions prevailing in the labor market, and the philosophies of management. The selection package, however, generally includes an application blank, an interview, the use of tests, and other selection tools such as a medical examination, personal references, and investigations by bonding companies.

The application blank normally asks for:

a) *Personal data* including the applicant's name, address, telephone number, sex, age, height, weight, health, marital status, and size of family.

b) *Education*, including schools attended, ad-

dresses, dates, programs majored in, and degrees received.

c) *Employment* record, including name of employer, address, dates of employment, job title and duties, salary earned, and reasons for leaving.

d) *Military service*, including branch of service, dates, rank, duties, special awards and citations, and type of discharge.

e) *Special activities*, including name of organization, dates, offices held, awards, and hobbies.

f) *References*, which usually include the names and addresses of former employers, teachers, doctors, ministers, and businessmen. Relatives and friends are normally excluded.

Most companies use an unweighted application blank, as illustrated in Figure 18–1, which gives a comprehensive picture of the applicant. Others, however, will sometimes use a weighted application blank which assigns points to various factors having a close relationship to successful selling.

The personal interview

Basically, there are two types of personal interviews: the *preliminary or screening* interview, which serves to weed out applicants who obviously are unsuited for the job, and the *secondary or follow-up* interview which is designed to obtain additional information from the applicant.

Interviews may be further distinguished as *planned* or *structured* versus *nondirective* or *in-*

formal. Group interviews are also used. The *planned* interview is very carefully organized on the basis of specific objectives, what types of information will be sought and given, how the interview will be conducted, and how much time will be spent in conducting it. The *nondirective* interview, on the other hand, is not organized and conducted in accordance with a list of predetermined objectives and questions. In this type of interview, the applicant is given the responsibility for determining the nature of the conversation. The advantages claimed for this type of interview are that the applicant is more likely to reveal his true self than he is in the planned interview, where he tends to give answers which he thinks the interviewer wants. It is also easier for the interviewee to relax. However, the nondirective interview may fail to secure answers to important questions, and sometimes the things an applicant doesn't talk about may be just as important as the items he mentions.

The *depth* interview is designed to obtain more complete and detailed information on specific questions. For example, a normal question to ask is what hobbies an applicant might have. In most instances, simply naming the hobby will suffice, but in the depth interview additional questions are asked such as:

Why do you like this particular hobby?
How did you get started in it?
Approximately how much time and money do you spend on it?
How does this hobby help you in your work?

The emphasis in the depth interview is on the "whys," and it is designed to obtain the person's reasons and feelings for doing something that might relate to his qualifications for selling.

Label each of the following statements as true or false.

_____ 1. The best way to increase corporate sales is to simply hire more salesmen.

_____ 2. Most companies use an unweighted application blank as part of the selection process.

_____ 3. Nondirective interviews are not organized in accordance with a list of predetermined objectives and questions.

_____ 4. Depth interviews are designed to find out such things as what hobbies the applicant might have, what other interests, and so on.

Now turn to Answer Frame 1[18] on page 116 to check your answers.

Frame 2[18]

The personal interview (continued)

In the *group* interview the applicant is interviewed by several persons at one time rather than by a single interviewer. This type of interview saves time and provides an opportunity for seeing how the applicant will respond and adapt to different types of persons. A disadvantage is that some applicants find it difficult to relax in the presence of several persons and may develop a defensive attitude, particularly if several persons are asking him questions that he thinks might be designed to trap him.

Another type of group interview is where several applicants are present at the same time, and all are interviewed by a single interviewer. Under this method, all the applicants get the same information under the same conditions. However, it is less personal, and the interviewer is unable to question each person as extensively as would be the case where each applicant is interviewed separately.

Most sales managers place considerable emphasis on the personal interview because it allows them to observe the personality traits of the candidate in a live and realistic manner. Questions frequently asked are:

Why do you wish to pursue a career in selling?
Why are you interested in our particular company?
What are your major strengths and weaknesses?

FIGURE 18–1

Application for sales position (page 1)

APPLICATION FOR SALES POSITION
(All information treated confidentially)

Date_____

Name (print)_____ Telephone number_____ Is this in your name?_____

Present address_____ How long have you lived there?_____
No.   Street   City   State   Zip

Previous address_____ How long did you live there?_____
No.   Street   City   State   Zip

Business address_____ Business telephone number_____
No.   Street   City   State   Zip

Date of birth_____19___
Check your State law as to discrimination because of age.
Height____ft.____in. Weight____lbs.
Are you a citizen of the U.S.? ☐ Yes, ☐ No

☐ Married; Date(s)_____
☐ Single, ☐ Engaged, ☐ Separated, ☐ Divorced
☐ Widowed. Date Sep., Div., Wid._____

No. children____ Their ages____
No. other dependents____ Ages____
Soc. Sec. No._____

Position applied for_____ Earnings expected $_____ Pay method preferred_____

Why are you applying to this Company?_____

Who referred you to this Company?_____ Names of relatives or friends employed by this Company_____

Have you ever applied to, or been employed by, this Company?_____ If so, when_____ Where?_____

EDUCATION

Type of School	Name of School	Courses Majored In	Check Last Year Completed				Graduate? Degrees Received	Last Year Attended
Elementary			5	6	7	8	☐ Yes, ☐ No	19
High School			1	2	3	4	☐ Yes, ☐ No	19
College			1	2	3	4		19
College			1	2	3	4		19
Business or Trade School			1	2	3	4		19
Other			1	2	3	4		19

JOBS WHILE IN SCHOOL AND DURING SUMMER

	Name of Employer	Your Job	Your Salary	Dates From	To	Hours Per Week
1.						
2.						
3.						
4.						

Scholastic standing in H. S._____ In College_____
(Designate top 25%, middle 50%, lowest 25%)

Favorite subjects_____ Least liked_____

EXTRACURRICULAR ACTIVITIES (exclude racial, religious, or nationality groups)

In high school_____ In college_____

Offices held_____ Offices held_____

Principal source of your spending money while in H. S. and College_____

Part of College expenses you earned: ☐ None, ☐ 0-25%, ☐ 25-50%, ☐ 50-75%, ☐ More than 75%_____

What scholarships or fellowships have you received?_____

What languages other than English do you speak?_____ Read?_____

What periodicals do you read regularly?_____

What hobbies do you have?_____

Form No. SA-101-R-2

Copyright, 1967, The Dartnell Corporation, Chicago, Ill. 60610. Printed in U. S. A.
Developed by The McMurry Company

Courtesy: Dartnell Corp.

FIGURE 18–1 (Continued)

Application for sales position (page 2)

WORK HISTORY

Include (a) self-employment and (b) secondary or moonlighting jobs (mark the latter with an asterisk)

Beginning with the most recent, list below the names and addresses of all your employers: a. Company name b. Address and telephone number	Kind of Business	Time Employed				How Was Job Obtained?	Nature of Work at Start
		From		To			
		Mo.	Yr.	Mo.	Yr.		
1. a. ___ b. ___							
2. a. ___ b. ___							
3. a. ___ b. ___							
4. a. ___ b. ___							
5. a. ___ b. ___							
6. a. ___ b. ___							
7. a. ___ b. ___							
8. a. ___ b. ___							

Indicate by number_____any of the above employees whom you do not wish us to contact.

In the last 5 years, how much time have you lost from work? (Illnesses, leave of absence, or other conditions)_____

Have you ever drawn unemployment compensation?_____Date(s)_____

Are you willing to furnish fidelity bond at our expense? ☐Yes, ☐No; if no, why not?_____

Please summarize specific experience below:

OVER-THE-COUNTER (retail) SELLING   Years_____For what firms?_____
Lines sold_____

DELIVERY SALES (e.g., a bakery route)   Years_____For what firms?_____
Lines sold_____

CALLING ON HOMES OR ROUTE SELLING (calling on the trade)   Years_____For what firms?_____
Lines sold_____

MISSIONARY SALES (e.g., pharmaceutical detailing, etc.)   Years_____For what firms?_____
Lines sold_____

TECHNICAL (e.g., engineering) SALES   Years_____For what firms?_____
Lines sold_____

SPECIALTY SALES OF TANGIBLES, e.g., BOOKS   Years_____For what firms?_____
Lines sold_____

SPECIALTY SALES OF INTANGIBLES, e.g., LIFE INSURANCE OR SERVICES   Years_____For what firms?_____
Lines sold_____

HIGH LEVEL (big ticket) SALES   Years_____For what firms?_____
Lines sold_____

MULTIPLE SELLING (where more than one person is involved in the buying decision)   Years_____For what firms?_____
Lines sold_____

Are you willing, if necessary, to do direct (door-to-door) selling?_____
Are you willing to work straight commission?_____
If necessary, are you willing to work nights?_____Saturdays?_____

Personal References (Not former employers or relatives)	Address	Phone Number
1.		
2.		
Bank Reference (give name and location)		

FIGURE 18–1 (*Continued*)

Application for sales position (page 3)

	Earnings Per Month at Start	Nature of Work at Leaving (State territory in which you worked)	Earnings Per Month at Leaving	Supervisory Positions Held	No. of People Supervised	Reasons for Leaving	Name of Immediate Supervisor
							Name ___ / Title ___
							Name ___ / Title ___
							Name ___ / Title ___
							Name ___ / Title ___
							Name ___ / Title ___
							Name ___ / Title ___
							Name ___ / Title ___
							Name ___ / Title ___

PERSONAL

Do you own your home? Value $_____, Mortgage $_____; Rent $_____, Board $_____, Live with relatives? $_____

Given name of spouse_____ Spouse's age_____. Is she (or he) employed? ☐ No, ☐ Yes, part-time

☐ Yes, full-time. Kind of work_____. Earnings $_____ per_____.

What sources of income do you have other than employment?_____

What do you owe now? Car $_____; Furniture, TV, etc. $_____; Other $_____

Life insurance carried by employer $_____; by yourself $_____; Accident $_____.

Father's occupation (or former occupation)_____ By whom were you raised?_____

Indicate: Brother(s)	Sister(s)	Age(s)	Occupation(s)
Brother___	Sister___		
Brother___	Sister___		
Brother___	Sister___		
Brother___	Sister___		

SPECIAL ACTIVITIES
(List past or present activities since leaving school)

Type of Organization	Name or Description of Organization	When Did You Actively Participate? From	To	Offices Held During Last Five Years	Average Time Now Given Per Week
Business or Professional Activities					
Lodges, Fraternities, Social Groups					
Civic or Community Organizations					
Other					

FIGURE 18–1 (Continued)

Application for sales position (page 4)

SERVICE IN U.S. ARMED FORCES

What is your current military service status?_____

If exempt or rejected, what was the reason?_____

Have you served in the U.S. Armed Forces? ☐ No, ☐ Yes; (If yes) Date active duty started_____19___

Which force? ☐ Army, ☐ Air Force, ☐ Navy, ☐ Marines, ☐ C. G.; What branch of that force?_____Starting rank_____

Overseas: Date(s)_____Location(s)_____

Date of discharge_____19___Type of discharge_____Rank at discharge_____

Were you hospitalized while in Service? ☐ No, ☐ Yes; (If yes) From_____19___to_____19___and from_____19___to_____19___

For what reason?_____What percent recovery?_____

What citations and awards have you received?_____

What special training did you receive?_____

What training have you taken (or do you plan to take) under the G. I. Bill?_____

How much pension or disability compensation are you eligible for or do you receive?_____For what reason?_____

HEALTH

What is your present physical condition?_____Smoking habits_____

What physical handicaps or limitations do you have?_____

Do you suffer from: Hay Fever_____Asthma_____Allergies? (list)_____

Have you had any form of stomach trouble, ulcers, colitis, etc.?_____

List serious illnesses, operations, accidents (other than auto), nervous disorders, and approximate dates_____

When did you last see a physician?_____Why?_____

Are you willing to take a physical exam at our expense? ☐ Yes, ☐ No.

TERRITORY PREFERENCES, TRAVEL, CAR OWNERSHIP

If your application is considered favorably,
on what date will you be available for work?_____19___How much notice will you require?_____Days

Territory preferred_____Why?_____

Is there any reason why you would not be willing to relocate?_____

How much time per month could you spend traveling?_____

Do you have full use of a car for your work? ☐ No, ☐ Yes; Make, model, and year of car(s) owned_____

What type of license do you have? ☐ Ordinary driver's, ☐ Chauffeur's; What state?_____What city?_____

Was your operator's permit ever suspended? ☐ No, ☐ Yes; if yes, why?_____

Auto accidents: Date(s)_____Describe fully_____

Automobile insurance: Collision $_____ Public liability $_____

OTHER STATEMENTS

Are there any other experiences, skills, or qualifications which you feel would especially fit you for work with this Company?

_____

What are your plans or aims for the future?_____

Signature_____

What do you want to be or become in 5, 10, 20 years from now?

What have you done to prepare yourself for a career in selling?

When the candidate answers these questions, both *what* he says and *how* he says it are evaluated in order to determine whether he has the necessary traits to succeed in selling.

Psychological tests

Special tests are widely used today in the selection process. The ones most commonly employed are intelligence, personality, interest, and sales aptitude tests.

Intelligence tests are designed to measure mental ability. The Otis Self-Administering Test of Mental Ability is one of the most frequently used tests of this type. Generally, companies will also attempt to differentiate between abstract or mechanical intelligence versus social intelligence because of the greater applicability of the latter type of intelligence in almost all types and levels of selling.

Personality tests attempt to measure the presence of such traits as self-confidence, independence, aggressiveness, self-reliance, ambition, emotional stability, optimism, and other similar traits closely related to success in selling. There are many different types of personality tests. One of the most widely used ones is the Bernreuter Personality Inventory published by the Stanford University Press.

Interest tests are designed to measure the extent to which a person will like or dislike the various activities connected with selling. The Strong Vocational Interest Blank and Kuder Preference Record are representative of this type of test.

Finally, there are *sales aptitude* tests which are designed to determine the capacity or latent ability a person has to become a successful salesman. Such characteristics as determination, persistence, and the desire to influence people are measured. An *achievement* test, on the other hand, measures the degree or level of competence a person has already achieved with regard to a given task or activity. In addition, there are many other specialized tests which are specifically designed for individual companies. These tests measure a person's degree of achievement in such related areas as arithmetic, bookkeeping, language ability, and so on.

In using tests in selecting applicants, it should be remembered that most testing procedures are based on averages or the "normal" type of employee. Though this information is helpful, it should not automatically eliminate persons who do not fit the stereotype and who might under certain circumstances become successful in selling. Another danger of testing is that it may eliminate highly creative people. Consequently, tests should be interpreted with great care and evaluated in relation to the other selection processes. Some tests are also very complex and may have to be administered and interpreted by a trained psychologist.

True or false?

_____ 1. Group interviews invariably consist of several interviewers and one candidate.

_____ 2. Considerable emphasis is placed on the personal interview in the selection process.

_____ 3. The Otis Self-Administering Test of Mental Ability, the Bernreuter Scale, and the Strong Vocational Blank are all psychological tests which are used in selecting sales personnel.

_____ 4. Various selection tests may be combined to eliminate any subjective evaluation on the part of management.

Now turn to Answer Frame 2[18] on page 116 to check your answers.

Answer frame 1[18]

1. False. Effective selling begins with selecting persons who have the potential and desire to sell and then training them properly. Simply hiring more men will not result in greater profits in the long run.
2. True. Most companies use an unweighted application blank, but others use a weighted blank which assigns points to various factors having a close relationship to success in selling.
3. True. The advantage of a nondirective interview is that the applicant is more likely to reveal his true self.
4. False. The emphasis in depth interviews is on the "whys," and it is designed to obtain the person's reasons and feelings for doing certain things.

If you missed any of the above, you should reread Frame 1[18] before turning to Frame 2[18] on page 110.

Answer frame 2[18]

1. False. Group interviews may be as described, but another group format would consist of *one* interviewer and *several* candidates.
2. True. The personal interview allows management to observe the personality traits of candidates in a live and realistic manner.
3. True. Companies generally use intelligence tests (Otis), personality tests (Bernreuter), interest tests (Strong), and a sales aptitude test in the selection process.
4. False. Though test information is helpful, it should not automatically eliminate persons who do not fit the stereotype and might be successful salesmen. Tests should be used with care and evaluated in relation to other selection processes.

If you missed any of the above, you should restudy Frame 2[18] before turning to Frame 3[18] below.

Frame 3[18]

Purposes of training

Training programs play a vital part in developing an effective sales force. In addition to motivating salesmen and increasing their productivity, these programs are also designed to decrease turnover, develop better morale, secure more effective control over the selling effort, improve customer relations, and help to reduce selling costs. The programs will also vary in relation to the amount of money available for training, the type of product or service being sold, and the experience of the salesmen. With new recruits, for example, an attempt will be made to achieve all of the latter objectives, whereas, with more experienced salesmen, the purpose of the program may be narrowed and aimed at introducing a new product or promotional program.

General content of training programs

Typical training program content covers:[1]

General company information including its history, organization, identification of executive personnel, policies, and promotion.

Company operating information including credit policies and practices, shipping, service, handling complaints, compensation plan, quotas, and control of expenses.

Product information including different product lines, manufacturing processes, product features, product uses, and prices.

Customer information including classification of customers, buying motives and habits, and special problems.

[1] Ibid., pp. 546–47.

Market information covering territory assignments, market potentials, routing procedures, general and local business conditions, and competition.

Sales training (as opposed to product training) which relates to all phases of the sales process such as:

Developing a selling personality.
Methods for prospecting.
Analyzing consumers.
Sales approaches.
Methods for organizing the sales presentation.
Communication and persuasion.
Handling objections.
Closing.
Building a customer following.
Methods for evaluating and improving both selling and nonselling duties.

Personnel used in training programs

Personnel used in training salesmen generally come from three sources: company-line executives, staff trainers, and outside consultants. *Company-line executives* are such persons as senior salesmen, field supervisors, and sales managers. The advantages of training by these people is that they are more familiar with the actual work and problems of the salesmen, and they themselves are generally highly successful in selling. The main drawbacks of using company-line executives are that they often are too busy and lack the time for such work. In addition, these people may be highly successful in selling, but this does not guarantee that they will be effective teachers.

Staff trainers are persons who are employed to serve as trainers and also persons recruited from other departments in the company. A professional sales trainer is usually well qualified to teach and is given sufficient time to develop training programs. A staff trainer does not have the authority of a line executive, and additional costs are incurred in maintaining a separate training department. The advantages of using persons drawn from other departments is that they can provide real expertise in areas related to selling, and their participation does not add much to the

cost of the training program. Again, however, these people are less familiar with actual selling, they often do not have adequate time, and they may or may not be good teachers.

Outside consultants can be obtained from firms and agencies which specialize in sales training. College professors who teach selling and sales management can also be used, as well as other recognized authorities on selling. These outside consultants are particularly appropriate for smaller and medium-sized firms which cannot afford the costs of having a full-time trainer. However, large companies also use outside consultants, since they often can do a more effective job of teaching various parts of the program. These outside consultants usually are experts in their field, are good teachers, and they have the latest information on selling and sales management. The major disadvantage of using such persons is that sometimes they are unable to relate as specifically as is desired to a particular product or service.

Methods for training

The five methods commonly used for conducting training programs are the lecture method, discussion, demonstrations, role playing, and on-the-job or field training.

Although the *lecture* method can cover a great deal of material over a relatively short period of time, it is not always appropriate for teaching certain areas of selling. For example, the lecture may be appropriate for telling salesmen how to secure prospects, but in teaching how to open or close the sale, other methods are generally more effective. The lecture method is also more appropriate for initial sales training programs rather than advanced or refresher courses. Consequently, it is usually more beneficial for new salesmen and of lesser value for experienced ones.

Discussion includes question and answer sessions, cases, round tables, and panels. This method has considerable flexibility, involves greater participation, and is generally more interesting. As a result, it has wide acceptance and is one of the most popular methods used for training salesmen. Its main weakness is that often it cannot be used with new or green salesmen, as they do not have the knowledge or experience to conduct intelligent and profitable discussions.

The *demonstration* is especially adaptive to selling because so much of selling relates to showing or actually demonstrating the product or service. Seeing is infinitely more effective than hearing, and also increases its likelihood of being remembered. The sales presentation can also be made easier to understand by using charts, slides, films, video tape recordings, and other visual aids.

Role playing consists of creating artificial but realistic situations which will simulate actual conditions in the field. Situations in everyday selling are acted out, thereby giving the student a better understanding of and feeling for the problems he will encounter. It is an excellent and effective method for training. Its major limitation is that role playing is more involved than it appears. Consequently, it can be good or bad depending upon the skill of the leader, and the ability of the participants to act out their roles in a realistic manner.

On-the-job training is used in the final stages of the training program. It involves actual calls in the field with the sales supervisor, trainer, or a senior salesman accompanying the new salesman to observe what he is doing. It is a practical and effective method for training which specifically relates to live and actual problems. Its main drawback is that it is very time consuming for the observers; however, this factor is insignificant in relation to the many other benefits that can be obtained from using this method.

In summary, there are several and uniquely different methods for training salesmen. Each has its respective advantages and disadvantages and most training programs will use a combination of methods.

Mistakes to avoid

One of the greatest mistakes in training is to underestimate its importance. Some sales managers feel that formalized training is unnecessary, as they believe that actual experience is the most important teacher. It cannot be denied that there is a close relationship between experience and successful selling. However, the increased costs and competition in selling make it necessary to minimize the errors that can be made by relying solely on experience. The salesman's work today is also more involved than it used to be and requires a higher level of education and training.

A second common error is to conduct training on a periodic or sporadic basis. It is sometimes assumed that if a man completes a training program, he will automatically remember and continue to practice what he has learned. Nothing is further from the truth; the very nature of selling requires that the salesman be motivated and trained on a continuing basis. A professional never stops learning or attempting to improve himself. Consequently, if selling is to become more professionalized and to fulfill its several objectives, then training must be continuous.

A third common mistake in training is for management to identify the problems and determine the purposes of the program with little or no consultation with the salesmen. Such an approach encounters resistance and is almost doomed from the start, for it fails to secure the participation of the very persons for whom the program is intended. Hence, if the program is to be realistic and effective, then it certainly should include the salesmen in the initial stages of determining the objectives and content of the program.

Label each of the following statements as true or false.

_____ 1. Line personnel such as senior salesmen are often used effectively to train new salesmen.

_____ 2. The lecture method of sales training is usually more beneficial for new salesmen than for experienced ones.

_____ 3. Role playing is a technique which tends to prevent salesmen from taking salesmanship training seriously.

_____ 4. Little formalized sales training is necessary because the best place to train salesmen is in the field.

Now turn to Answer Frame 3¹⁸ on page 120 to check your answers.

Answer frame 3¹⁸

1. True. The advantage of using field men is that they are generally successful in selling, but they are often too busy to do such training work.
2. True. The lecture method may be appropriate for *telling* salesmen *what* to do, but in explaining *how* to do it other methods generally are more effective.
3. False. Role playing is a serious approach to salesmanship. It actually consists of creating artificial sales situations giving the sales student a feeling of the problems he will encounter in the field and an opportunity to practice making presentations.
4. False. The increased costs and competition in selling make it necessary to minimize the errors made in the field by inexperienced salesmen without proper training.

If you missed any of the above, you should reread Frame 3¹⁸. You should now turn to page 125 to work the Second Review, which covers Chapters 10–18. Then work the Final Examination on page 129, which covers the entire PLAID.

First review: Chapters 1–9, inclusive

1. During which of the following periods did our capacity to produce begin to exceed our ability to sell goods?
   a) 1800 to 1850
   b) 1850 to 1900
   c) 1900 to 1950

2. Selling and advertising are the only two business functions which generate direct revenues and profits. (T or F)

3. Under present social and economic conditions, it is impossible for selling to become a science. (T or F)

4. Successful selling means getting the order. (T or F)

5–6. With reference to successful selling traits, (5) _____ is a feeling of strongly liking something and being fervently absorbed in it, and (6) _____ is believing you can achieve what you wish to accomplish.

7. The number of calls a salesman makes will generally equal the number of sales he makes. (T or F)

8. Methods for paying salesmen are generally more varied than in other types of jobs. (T or F)

9. The need for selling is not a universal activity and generally varies from one geographic area to another. (T or F)

10. If a salesman can sell one product or service well, with a little training he is generally capable of selling other products or services. (T or F)

11. _____ is a study of the drives, urges, desires, or wants which influence a person to buy a particular product or service.

12. A _____ motive relates to consumer decisions involved in choosing a product or service with a particular brand name.

13. Products which are frequently consumed on a daily or weekly basis, are available in many stores which are located near the consumer, are competitively priced, and are generally intensively advertised are referred to as _____ goods.

14. Products with very special and unique characteristics and ones for which there generally are no substitutions are referred to as _____ goods.

15. With reference to motivation, the _____-_____ theory maintains that the buyer's mind passes through five successive stages (attention, interest, desire, action, and satisfaction) during the buying process.

16. The _____-_____ theory of motivation states that the wants, needs, or problems of the buyer should be the salesman's frame of reference, and he gears his presentation to showing how his product or service will solve these problems.

17. A salesman should be positive minded and, therefore, should learn about the advantages of his product rather than its disadvantages or limitations. (T or F)

18. A salesman should be optimistic and confident, but this does not mean that he should

avoid learning about his competitor's products. (T or F)

19. Advertising is geared to the masses, while personal salesmanship is geared to specific individuals. (T or F)

20. With reference to opening a personal credit account the three C's generally considered are *capital, collateral,* and *character.* (T or F)

21. A _____-_____ price is used when a manufacturer ships to buyers in different locations but charges all of them the same price regardless of the distance involved.

22. The shipping term "f.o.b. destination" means that the buyer incurs the transportation charges from the seller's place of business to the final destination point. (T or F)

23. Of the states which now have fair-trade laws, price maintenance contracts are now enforceable in:
    a) None
    b) 16
    c) 27
    d) 36
    e) All of the states

24. The Truth-in-Lending Act of 1968 requires that credit terms be stated in a standard way and also establishes maximum interest rates. (T or F)

25. Some companies sell their products to different types of distributors and will grant them _____ discounts depending upon their classification and the services they perform.

26. Under the "cold turkey" method of prospecting, the salesman does not carefully preselect his prospects and under the "cold canvas," method, a limited criteria is used. (T or F)

27. One of the advantages or strengths of using the telephone in selling is that the salesman can pick his prospects directly from the telephone book without having to select them in accordance with some predetermined criteria. (T or F)

28. It generally is not wise to attempt to close most sales by telephone. (T or F)

29. Charts, graphs, and illustrations should be used with care in a presentation, for sometimes they can be overused and serve to distract the prospect. (T or F)

30. All prospective buyers seek benefits—that is why they are interested in buying a particular product or service. (T or F)

31. The main senses for a salesman to appeal to are the senses of hearing and seeing. To refer to the other senses often results in confusing or distracting the prospect. (T or F)

32. The organizational pattern for lengthy sales presentations generally should be varied in order to avoid making the presentation too mechanical and boring. (T or F)

33. In those cases where the prospect takes control of the interview, the salesman has nothing to worry about for it shows that the prospect is interested in the product or service. (T or F)

34. It is generally good procedure for the salesman to secure agreement on one point before proceeding to another. (T or F)

35. After a sale is made, it is no longer necessary for the salesman to show any further interest in the customer. (T or F)

36. A prospect should never be approached by a salesman unless the salesman has complete information on him. (T or F)

37. It is not always necessary for the salesman to make an appointment before calling on a prospect. (T or F)

Now check your answers with those appearing on page 124.

Answers to first review

1. C
2. False
3. True
4. False
5. Enthusiasm
6. Confidence
7. False
8. True
9. False
10. True

11. Motivation
12. Selective
13. Convenience
14. Specialty
15. Mental-states
16. Problem-solution
17. False
18. True
19. True
20. False

21. Basing-point
22. False
23. B
24. False
25. Trade (could also be *functional*)
26. False
27. False
28. True
29. True

30. True
31. False
32. True
33. False
34. True
35. False
36. False
37. True

Now turn to Chapter 10 on page 47.

Second review:
Chapters 10–18, inclusive

1. When the prospect raises objections, it always shows that he is not interested in the product or service the salesman is attempting to sell. (T or F)
2. All objections should be answered immediately, for if the salesman delays in giving an answer he generally will annoy the prospect. (T or F)
3. Sometimes the prospect will raise an objection which does not warrant a serious answer by the salesman. (T or F)
4. The correct time to close a sale generally is when the buyer has indicated he is ready to buy. (T or F)
5. The most accurate closing signal is generally the prospect's comments. (T or F)
6. The salesman should let the prospect set the pace and also control the presentation. (T or F)
7. The "alternative choice" method of closing does not ask the prospect if he wishes to buy but assumes that he wants to and is ready to buy. (T or F)
8. Prospects generally respond favorably to two-man closes because they feel they are getting more attention. (T or F)
9. Many prospects look for variety of selection when buying a product. This means that the salesman should show the prospect as many styles or models of a particular product as he possibly can. (T or F)
10. The salesman should fit the sale to the customer even if it means selling less than the customer thinks he needs, or in some cases not selling him at all. (T or F)
11. After a product or service has been sold, the salesman should be careful about offering additional advice or helpful hints because many customers will interpret this as an attempt to sell them more merchandise. (T or F)
12. If the salesman has served the customer well and sold him the appropriate product or service, it generally is not necessary to thank him for his patronage. (T or F)
13. The question of ethics in selling becomes more relevant when the market is competitive and it is more difficult to secure sales. (T or F)
14. The salesman's only responsibility to his competitors is that he attempt to outsell them. (T or F)
15. Inasmuch as selling is such an important activity, a single code of ethics has been established for selling. (T or F)
16. What would the salesman's performance index be if his expected sales were $30,000 for a given period of time and his actual sales amounted to $45,000 at the end of this period?
17. In general, how much of the salesman's total time is spent in face-to-face selling?

    a) 5 percent
    b) 10 percent
    c) 15 percent
    d) 20 percent
    e) 25 percent

18. What the salesman does outside his work of selling is his own personal business, and these outside activities generally have little or no effect upon his work. (T or F)

19. Retail selling in comparison with other types of selling tends to place more emphasis on buying by the customer versus selling by the salesman. (T or F)

20. In suggesting related items, the salesman usually should not suggest more than one or two items because mentioning more than this number might be interpreted as high-pressure selling. (T or F)

21. If the store does not have the item requested by the customer, the salesman in a tactful manner should belittle the item requested and aggressively attempt to sell him a substitute item. (T or F)

22. A "just-looking" type of customer generally should be left alone to look at the merchandise. (T or F)

23. In handling a "confused" type of customer, the salesman generally should refrain from asking too many questions, for this may further confuse the customer. (T or F)

24. When dealing with a "quiet" customer, it is good practice for the salesman to speak louder in order to get him to say something. (T or F)

25. Most industrial companies tend to buy from more than one industrial salesman. (T or F)

26. _____ is a term which refers to the practice of buying from a particular company because it buys from you.

27. The industrial salesman generally has fewer accounts than the salesman of consumer products. (T or F)

28. There is a tendency for purchasing agents to buy more on the basis of emotion than reason when prices become more competitive and product qualities become more identical. (T or F)

29. Management of salesmen often receives more attention than the management of other types of business personnel. (T or F)

30. A sales _____ is an estimate of the sales that will be made for a particular period of time such as a season or a year.

31. Sales _____ are dollar amounts that the salesman is expected to sell in a given territory for a given period of time.

32. With reference to compensating salesmen, under the _____ _____ plan the salesman is paid a fixed amount on a weekly or monthly basis.

33. Approximately 60 percent of the sales managers use a combination salary and incentive plan for compensating salesmen. (T or F)

34. Because of the uncertainties involved, the bonus plan generally has less incentive value than other methods for compensating salesmen. (T or F)

35. A nondirective interview is not organized in accordance with a list of predetermined objectives and questions, and the applicant also is given the responsibility for determining the nature of the conversation. (T or F)

36. An _____ test is designed to determine the capacity or latent ability a person has to become a successful salesman.

37. With reference to sales training, _____ _____ is a method of training whereby artificial but realistic situations are used to stimulate actual conditions in the field.

Now check your answers with those appearing on page 128.

Answers to second review

1. False	11. False	21. False	31. Quotas
2. False	12. False	22. True	32. Straight salary
3. True	13. True	23. True	33. True
4. True	14. False	24. False	34. True
5. True	15. False	25. True	35. True
6. False	16. 150 percent	26. Reciprocity	36. Aptitude
7. True	17. D	27. True	37. Role playing
8. False	18. False	28. True	
9. False	19. True	29. True	
10. True	20. True	30. Forecast	

Final examination (74 objective questions): Chapters 1–18, inclusive

1. Selling as a function of business began as early as:

    a) 1000 B.C.
    b) 2000 B.C.
    c) 3000 B.C.
    d) 4000 B.C.
    e) 5000 B.C.

2. The two major objectives of the "marketing concept" are satisfying the consumer and profitable sales. (T or F)

3. Personality is an important aspect of selling, and if a person is not born with a "selling personality" it is impossible for him to be successful in selling. (T or F)

4. Having the "right mental attitude" means to look and act intelligent. (T or F)

5. _____ is a selling trait of a successful salesman. It means "putting yourself in the other fellow's shoes" or having a sensitivity to the feelings and interests of others.

6. It generally is easier to teach a salesman how to speak effectively than it is to teach him how to be creative. (T or F)

7. In selling, the ability to communicate means getting the prospect to understand you. (T or F)

8. In many types of selling, the salesman has complete freedom in determining when he will work, where he will work, how long, whom he will call on, and what he will do. (T or F)

9. The various types of selling jobs are relatively easy to classify. (T or F)

10. To what extent did the number of persons in selling increase over the general population during the period from 1890 to 1968?

    a) 5 times
    b) 10 times
    c) 17 times
    d) 19 times
    e) 25 times
    f) Over 30 times

11. A _____ motive refers to those particular factors which motivate a person to choose one general type of product or service over another.

12. A _____ motive refers to consumer decisions regarding the particular retailer or dealer from whom a product or service will be purchased.

13. Products with a relatively high unit value which are consumed infrequently, which are available in less convenient outlets, and which generally involve careful planning and comparisons by the consumer are referred to as _____ goods.

14. A positive appeal is always better than a negative appeal. (T or F)

15. The _____-_____ theory of motivation maintains that the buyer makes a number of separate decisions or responses to the appeals or stimuli presented by the salesman.

16. Learning may be defined as the ability to retain information in the mind. (T or F)

17. It often takes the salesman a long time to learn about a product or service, but once it is

learned such knowledge remains permanent and continued study is unnecessary. (T or F)

18. Advertising helps to presell the consumer but is of little or no use in the sales presentation itself. (T or F)

19. Advertising can stimulate new interest and increased motivation in both the consumer and the salesman himself. (T or F)

20. There are many reasons why consumers fail to pay for a product or service, with deliberate dishonesty generally accounting for a comparatively small percentage of the total reasons. (T or F)

21. A _____-_____ price is a price established by contract between a manufacturer of a branded product and a wholesaler or retailer. The manufacturer decides what the minimum price should be, and the wholesaler or retailer may not sell below this established price.

22. The shipping term "c.i.f." means cost on imported freight. (T or F)

23. The Miller-Tydings Act of 1937 did not specifically recognize the nonsigner's clause and thus it put an end to control of prices at which nonsigners of price maintenance contracts could resell goods brought in from other states, even if the state law had such a clause. (T or F)

24. Better Business Bureaus have the power to make actual arrests. (T or F)

25. Quantity discounts may be granted on the basis of:
    a) The number of total units purchased.
    b) The dollar value of the order.
    c) The size of the package ordered.
    d) Bonus goods wherein the customer receives free merchandise or extra units depending upon the quantity ordered.
    e) Most of the above situations, but not all of them.
    f) All of the above situations.

26. Prospecting is an effective means for increasing sales, and the salesman need not worry that the amount of time spent in prospecting will hurt his total sales. (T or F)

27. Material presented over the telephone by the salesman should be just as well planned and organized as material presented in a face-to-face interview. (T or F)

28. To be effective, direct-mail selling should be based on a prospect list which is current and up to date. (T or F)

29. In order to control the presentation, the salesman generally should do more talking than the prospect. (T or F)

30. In many presentations the salesman should ask the prospect certain questions to make sure he is following or agreeing with him. (T or F)

31. Giving a sales presentation is very much like giving a speech. (T or F)

32. A salesman should never approach a prospect whom he feels he is bothering. (T or F)

33. If the salesman has gathered complete information about the prospect, he need not worry that he will have problems in making the first call. (T or F)

34. Whether an appointment with a prospect should be made or not is a personal matter which will vary with the product or service being sold and the circumstances surrounding the buying environment. (T or F)

35. A "mnemonic" word is a word which symbolizes the meaning of several words or a series of key ideas. (T or F)

36. An analogy is a comparison between two qualities made by using the words "like" or "as." (T or F)

37. The technique of periodically repeating and reviewing to make certain the prospect understands and agrees with the salesman should only be used with prospects who are confused. (T or F)

38. In those cases, where the objection raised by the prospect is a legitimate one, the salesman should not be afraid to admit the objection. (T or F)

39. "Denying the objection" is one of the most common methods used for answering objections. (T or F)

40. It is generally better to let the prospect, rather than the salesman himself, raise the objection, for this provides the prospect with an oppor-

tunity to participate in the presentation. (T or F)

41. The close should not be looked upon as a separate part of the sales process which should always be executed at the end of the presentation. (T or F)

42. Most sales are closed on the first attempted close. (T or F)

43. All selling points relating to a product or service should be mentioned by the salesman before a close is attempted. (T or F)

44. Normally the salesman should secure agreement on minor parts before proceeding to major or more critical points. (T or F)

45. The "direct appeal" is a very common method for closing. (T or F)

46. If the salesman has done an effective job and still fails to close the sale, he should insist on knowing why the prospect will not buy. (T or F)

47. Even if the customer is sold the appropriate product or service, he sometimes becomes dissatisfied with it. (T or F)

48. The first thing the salesman should do in handling a complaint is to inform the customer of the company's general policies for handling complaints. (T or F)

49. Helpful hints or advice should never be given to a prospect unless they relate directly to the product or service the salesman is selling. (T or F)

50. _____ ethics are fixed and always apply, regardless of the circumstances that prevail.

51. _____ ethics, on the other hand, are more flexible and adaptable to varying circumstances.

52. "Plateauing" or a decline in sales is a situation which often applies to inexperienced salesmen rather than seasoned ones. (T or F)

53. There generally is greater opportunity for the salesman to increase his sales by securing new accounts than by selling more to accounts he already has. (T or F)

54. Management generally has explicit policies regarding expenses incurred by salesmen. (T or F)

55. It is a misconception to believe that as a person grows older, it is normal for him to gain weight. (T or F)

56. The _____ approach is used a great deal in retail selling. It is an approach where the salesman refers to the major features of his product or service rather than using a greeting.

57–58–59. If the salesman at the beginning of a sale does not know the prospect's needs or what he can afford, it is usually advisable to start with the _____ price, then go to the _____ price if possible, and then to the _____ price if necessary.

60. In handling a "know-it-all" type of customer, the salesman generally should attempt to discourage his comments. (T or F)

61. In dealing with a "think-it-over" type of customer, it is good procedure for the salesman to ask him what additional points he wishes to have explained. (T or F)

62. The channels of distribution in industrial markets are usually longer than channels for consumer products. (T or F)

63. The manufacturer of an industrial product generally has fewer salesmen than a manufacturer of consumer products. (T or F)

64. The major buying motives of the purchasing agent generally are quality, service, and brand name. (T or F)

65. The industrial salesman generally does not attempt to sell a product or service on his first call. (T or F)

66. The fact that a man has been the number one salesman on the staff guarantees that he will be the best candidate for a sales manager's job. (T or F)

67. A limitation of the "sales force summary" method of making a sales forecast is that it is quite time consuming. (T or F)

68. Activity quotas are based on points rather than dollar or unit value. (T or F)

69. With reference to compensating salesmen, under the _____ _____ plan the salesman is paid according to his performance or the amount he sells.

70. Guaranteed draws do not have to be repaid if the salesman's commissions for the period are less than the draw. (T or F)

71. The most popular and widely used plan for paying the expenses of salesmen is a variation of the unlimited reimbursement plan, where the salesman is required to submit an itemized report of his expenses which must be examined and approved. (T or F)

72. A _____ interview is designed to obtain more complete and detailed information on specific questions.

73. An _____ test is designed to measure the extent to which a person will like or dislike the various activities connected with selling.

74. Most sales managers place little emphasis on the personal interview because it does not allow them to observe the personality traits of a candidate in a realistic manner. (T or F)

Now refer to page 134 to check your answers.

Answers to final examination

1. D	19. True	38. True	57. Middle
2. True	20. True	39. False	58. Higher
3. False	21. Fair-trade	40. False	59. Lower
4. False	22. False	41. True	60. False
5. Empathy	23. True	42. False	61. True
6. True	24. False	43. False	62. False
7. False	25. F	44. True	63. True
8. True	26. False	45. False	64. False
9. False	27. True	46. False	65. True
10. D	28. True	47. True	66. False
11. Primary	29. True	48. False	67. True
12. Patronage	30. True	49. False	68. True
13. Shopping	31. False	50. Absolute	69. Straight commission
14. False	32. False	51. Relative	70. True
15. Appeal-response or buying-decisions	33. False	52. False	71. True
16. False	34. True	53. True	72. Depth
17. False	35. True	54. True	73. Interest
18. False	36. False	55. True	74. False
	37. False	56. Merchandise	

You have now completed this PLAID on salesmanship.

Absolute ethics—Ethics which are constant and always apply, regardless of the circumstances that might prevail.

Achievement test—Test which measures the degree or level of competence a person has already achieved with regard to a given task or activity.

Acquired want—A want that is learned and which also is a further refinement of a basic want.

Activity quota—A quota which is based on points assigned to various selling activities rather than dollar or unit volume.

Advertising discount—A discount in the form of an advertising allowance based on the amount and type of merchandise bought.

Analogy—An example or illustration which relates one situation or circumstance with another.

Antimerger Act—An act passed in 1950 and designed to prevent the lessening of competition by making it more difficult for large companies to acquire other large or even medium-sized companies in their own or closely related markets.

"Appeal-response" theory—A theory which states that the buyer makes a number of separate decisions in response to the appeals or stimuli presented by the salesman.

Aptitude test—A test designed to determine the capacity or latent ability a person has to accomplish a given task.

Attitude—A person's state of mind, feeling, or disposition toward something.

Basic want—A want which is common to all human beings.

Basing-point price—A price determined from a given location or base point.

Benefit-proof technique—A technique used by the salesman where any benefit he mentions in connection with his product or service is always followed or supported with a specific proof.

Bonus—A lump sum of money given to the salesman at the end of a given period for performance which was above average or beyond a predetermined goal.

"Buying-decisions" theory—A theory which states that the buyer makes a number of separate decisions in response to the appeals or stimuli presented by the salesman.

Cash discount—A discount which is designed to encourage and reward early or prompt payment.

C.i.f. price—An abbreviation meaning "cost, insurance, and freight" which is used in export selling.

Clayton Act—An act passed in 1914 which broadened the latitude of the Sherman Antitrust Act.

C.l. discount—A discount given to a buyer for having bought a full "carload lot."

Close—The culminating stage of the sales process in which the prospect decides whether or not he will buy the product or service.

"Cold turkey" or "cold canvas" selling—A method of prospecting where the salesman does not select prospects in accordance with a predetermined criterion.

Convenience good—A product which is frequently consumed on a daily or weekly basis, is available in many stores which are located near the consumer, is competitively priced, and is generally intensively advertised. Such products as cigarettes, gasoline, or toothpaste are examples of a convenience good.

Credit—Permission to buy a product immediately and pay for it later.

Customer reference prospecting—A method of prospecting in which the salesman attempts to obtain the names of additional prospects from persons he has interviewed or customers who have purchased from him.

Daily plan—An outline and schedule of the things a salesman plans to accomplish on a given day.

Depth interview—A very complete type of interview which seeks "in depth" answers to questions.

Derived demand—A demand for a particular material or commodity which is dependent upon its end market use by the ultimate consumer.

Dyadic interaction—An integrated analysis of the roles played by both parties in a sale. It is an analysis where two separate units are treated as one.

Early order discount—A discount designed to encourage the buyer to order early in the season.

Emotional motive—A motive based on feelings which also is highly impulsive and not carefully planned in advance.

Ethics—Practices or principles for achieving ideal behavior or character.

Fair-trade price—A price established by contract between a manufacturer of a branded product and a wholesaler or retailer. The manufacturer decides what the minimum price will be and the wholesaler or retailer may not sell below this established price.

F.a.s. price—An abbreviation meaning "free alongside." The seller agrees to pay the transportation charges for getting the goods within reach of the loading cranes, and at this point title passes to the buyer.

Federal Trade Commission Act—An act passed in 1914 which established the Federal Trade Commission, giving it the power to investigate and to issue cease and desist orders in cases involving unfair methods of competition.

Flat expense allowance—Under this system the salesman, instead of having a given percent of his commission to cover expenses, is paid a flat dollar amount each day or week.

F.o.b. price—"Free on board" a railroad car, a ship, a plane, or a motor truck. Under this price the seller assumes the transportation charges to a given shipping point, and the buyer incurs the costs beyond that point.

Group discount—A discount given to a group of buyers who pool or combine their purchases into a single order.

Guaranteed draw—An advance payment of money to the salesman which does not have to be repaid if the salesman's commissions for the period are less than the draw.

Guaranteed price—A price which protects the buyer from any further price decreases that might occur prior to the time the product is either used or resold to the ultimate consumer.

Intelligence test—A test designed to measure a person's mental ability.

Interest test—A test designed to measure the extent to which a person will like or dislike the various activities connected with a given type of work.

Law of effect—A law related to learning which refers to repetition of a satisfactory response.

Law of exercise—A law related to learning which refers to a form of conditioning which elicits a second identical response to a specific stimulus if the first response has been rewarding or satisfying to the person.

Law of readiness—A law related to learning which refers to a person's ability and willingness to solve a problem.

L.c.l.—An abbreviation meaning "less than car load lot."

Learning—Any change in a person's response or behavior.

List price—A quoted or published price from which buyers are normally allowed discounts.

"Marketing concept"—A philosophy for doing business which emphasizes two basic objectives—consumer satisfaction and profitable sales.

"Mental-states" theory—A theory which maintains that the buyer's mind passes through successive stages during the buying process. These stages are "attention, interest, desire, action, and satisfaction."

Merchandise approach—An opening or greeting in which the salesman refers to a selling point related to the product which the prospect is examining or handling.

Metaphor—A word or phrase which refers to an object or idea in place of another by way of suggesting a comparative likeness.

Miller-Tydings Act—An act passed in 1937 which recognized that all dealers in a fair-trade state had to agree to price maintenance as long as one dealer had entered into such an agreement.

Mixed car-lot—A discount allowing the buyer to buy in smaller quantities rather than full car or truck lots of one product. Under this system, the buyer receives a balanced assortment of products and still receives a car load price.

Motivation—The study of the drives, urges, desires, or wishes which influence a person to buy a particular product or service.

Negative motive—A motive based on negative associations which emphasizes the problems or dangers a person will avoid by using a particular product or service.

Net price—The final price after all discounts and allowances have been deducted.

Nonguaranteed draw—An advance payment of money to the salesman which has to be repaid if the salesman's commissions for the period are less than the draw.

Patronage motive—Those considerations which cause a person to choose a particular dealer or retailer over another.

Perception—The process of becoming aware of something through the senses of seeing, hearing, touching, tasting, smelling, and internal sensing.

Personality test—A test which attempts to measure the degree to which a person possesses certain traits such as self-confidence, aggressiveness, enthusiasm, and so on.

Persuasion—The art of being able to change someone's thinking about something and also getting him to act on it.

Point system—A variation of the salary plus commission method for compensating salesmen. Under this system the salesman is rewarded with points for various types of accomplishments.

Positive motive—A motive based on positive associations or benefits which the consumer will receive from using the product or service.

Postage-stamp delivered price—Pricing method used when a company wishes to sell its product or service at the same price throughout its entire market.

Primary motive—Those particular factors which motivate a person to choose one general type of product or service over another.

"Problem-solution" theory—A theory which states that the wants, needs, or problems of the buyer serve as the salesman's frame of reference, and he gears his presentation to showing how his product or service will fulfill these wants or solve these problems.

Program presentation—A presentation which is organized and prepared on the basis of a careful survey of the buyer's needs.

Prospecting—Methods used by a salesman to find new customers.

Pure Food and Drug Act—An act passed in 1906 regulating the production, processing, and distribution of foods and drugs sold in interstate commerce.

Quantity discount—A discount for buying in large quantities.

Rational motive—A motive based on objective analysis and careful reasoning.

Reciprocity—A practice of buying from those who buy from you.

Reinforcement—A learning condition which increases the probability of an identical response, or a rewarding or satisfying situation which helps to stimulate the occurrence of the same response.

Relative ethics—Ethics which are flexible and adaptable to varying circumstances.

Resale price maintenance laws—Laws which make it legal for the manufacturer to set or control the price at which his product will be sold in the retail market.

Right mental attitude—An attitude which emphasizes the positive aspects of a situation rather than its negative points.

Robinson-Patman Act—An act passed in 1936 to protect small businesses by regulating price discrimination on products bought by retailers.

Role playing—Using artificial but realistic situations to simulate actual conditions.

Sales force summary—A forecast arrived at by estimates received from the salesmen and other sales executives.

Sales forecast—An estimate of the sales that will be made for a particular period of time such as a season or year.

Sales quota—Dollar amounts that a salesman is expected to sell in a given territory for a given period of time.

Sales spotters—Persons used for prospecting who receive cash or premium rewards from the salesman if the lead they provided him results in a sale.

Selective motive—Those factors causing a person to choose one brand name over another in the same product class.

Sherman Antitrust Act—Act passed in 1890 for the purpose of preventing monopolies and restraint of trade.

Shopping good—A product which is infrequently consumed in comparison with a convenience good, is available in fewer outlets which are generally located farther away from the consumer. Greater variances exist in price and quality, it has a higher unit value, and there is usually considerable planning by the consumer before he purchases such a product. Examples of shopping goods are a suit, a sport jacket, an appliance, furniture, and an automobile.

Showmanship—Methods used by the salesman to emphasize and dramatize selling points.

Simile—A comparison between two objects or ideas by using the words "like" or "as."

Specialty good—A product which has very special and unique characteristics. The consumer generally will "go out of his way" to purchase such a product and usually is reluctant to accept substitutes.

State fair-trade laws—Laws aimed at excessive price cutting of trademarked or branded merchandise and making it legal for the manufacturer to set or control the price at which his product will be sold in the retail market.

Substitution selling—An attempt by the salesman to

sell merchandise other than the specific type requested by the customer.

Suggestion selling—An attempt by the salesman to sell additional merchandise after the prospect has already made a purchase.

Testimonial prospecting—A method of prospecting where the salesman uses the names of well known and/or influential people to help him in selling to others.

Trade or functional discount—A discount granted by the seller on the basis of the buyer's trade classification and the functions or services he performs.

"Trading up"—An attempt by the salesman to get the prospect to buy the more expensive or better quality merchandise.

Truth-in-Lending Act—An act passed in 1968 which requires that credit terms be stated in a standard and meaningful way allowing the buyer to make comparisons.

Unfair trade practice laws—Laws varying from state to state, but generally prohibiting price cutting below a specified level which usually is set at approximately 6 percent above the invoice price.

User's expectation forecast—A forecast arrived at by asking consumers or customers what and how much they plan to buy for a given period.

Visualization—The process of picturing how something will look without actually seeing it.

Wheeler-Lea Act—An act passed in 1938 which prevents retailers from engaging in deceptive acts or practices in pricing.

Zone price—An equalized price for a product sold in different zones or geographical areas.

INDEX